THE AI-READY HUMAN

THE AI-READY HUMAN

YOUR 90-DAY PROGRAM TO STAY RELEVANT AS TECHNOLOGY
TRANSFORMS WORK

PAUL SLATER

BOUNDARY ASH
PRESS

The AI-Ready Human: Your 90-Day Program to Stay Relevant as Technology Transforms Work

Paul Slater

Published by Boundary Ash Press

Disclaimer: The information provided in this book is for educational and informational purposes only. While the author has made every effort to ensure accuracy, the rapidly evolving nature of AI technology means some information may become outdated. The strategies and advice offered are based on the author's experience and research but may not be suitable for every individual or situation. Readers should use their own judgment and, where appropriate, consult with professionals before implementing any strategies discussed in this book.

ISBN: 979-8-9945089-0-9 (hardcover)

ISBN: 979-8-9945089-1-6 (hardcover - deluxe)

ISBN: 979-8-9945089-2-3 (paperback)

eISBN: 979-8-9945089-3-0

First Edition

Cover design by Abdenasser Nejraoui

Interior design by the author

Printed in the United States of America

CONTENTS_

FOREWORD_

By Kyle McDowell, Bestselling Author of Begin With WE

I first met Paul Slater when I was a guest on his podcast, *Humanity Working*. It didn't take long for me to realize that we were aligned on a fundamental belief: our work—what we do for a living—should mean something. We shouldn't merely exist at work; we should thrive.

That conversation turned into a collaboration. Paul and his team expanded the concepts from my first book, *Begin With WE*, to build an online masterclass that brings my book's principles, the 10 WEs, to life. Together, we built something I would describe as unique, human, and wildly useful for leaders at all levels—the same words I would use to describe this book.

The AI-Ready Human isn't a book about "AI." It's a book about being human at a moment when technology is advancing faster than our ability to pause, reflect, and ask the right questions.

AI is here, and it isn't going anywhere. It isn't hype. It isn't a fad. AI has already changed (and will continue to change) how we work, how we communicate, and how decisions are made. Indeed, artificial intelligence has never been more powerful or ubiquitous. But with that power comes a quiet pressure to keep up. Because AI is transforming everything we do at a blistering pace, many people feel like they're falling behind.

If that last sentence resonates, this is the book for you.

The AI-Ready Human is a brilliantly structured, 90-day journey designed to help you stay relevant, grounded, and effective in a world that's evolving faster than most of us were trained for.

I've been privileged to lead tens of thousands of employees around the world in some of the most complex environments in business. And if there's one thing I know to be true, it's this: people who capitalize on and win through disruption aren't always the smartest or the most experienced. They're the most flexible and open to change. They're not married to "this is how it's always been done." They stay grounded while the ground is moving. They lead with courage, clarity, and care—even when (especially when) everything is changing.

If you think AI has already changed the world, you ain't seen nothing yet. It will continue to get faster, more capable, and more ingrained into everything we do. Any other conclusion is naïve. So we're left with a choice: resist the AI tsunami and be left behind, or embrace change as an opportunity and lead with it.

With or without AI, we must lead with care, courage, energy, and sound judgment. We need the ability to connect, to reflect, to challenge assumptions, and to change course when needed. We need to know how to capitalize on our strengths and address our opportunities and blind spots. We need to know when to trust the machine—and when to trust ourselves. And that's the gift of this book.

Over the next 90 days, you'll learn skills you probably didn't even know you needed: prompt clarity, judgment filters, energy management, verification instincts, and resilience. You'll engage in daily practices that will turn insight into action. You'll test ideas, reflect honestly, stretch your comfort zone, and grow.

And if you commit—not just to reading, but to doing—you'll come out the other side more capable and more prepared than most of the workforce.

You'll also come away with something even more important: a deeper sense of purpose. Because this book isn't about becoming more productive for productivity's sake. It's about becoming more human at a time when humanity matters more than ever.

Make no mistake: *The AI-Ready Human* will challenge you. But it will also equip and encourage you. Most importantly, it will help you become someone who isn't bracing for the future—because you're too busy shaping it.

Commit to this book. Make it part of your daily rhythm by practicing the valuable teachings within.

AI's impact on the workplace has very little to do with what most pundits would have you believe. The future isn't about AI versus humans. It's AI with humans.

Welcome to the future.

— **Kyle McDowell** Author of The Wall Street Journal and USA Today bestseller, *Begin With WE- 10 Principles for Building and Sustaining a Culture of Excellence.*

INTRODUCTION_

Whether you are a CEO or just starting out in the workplace, your job is changing. Perhaps only a little each day, but over the months and years, those changes are adding up.

If you aren't sure that's true, don't look forward – look back. Think about what you did before Generative AI like ChatGPT arrived. The chances are that the what, when, where, how, and possibly even the why of work were different for you.

And the rate of change is only likely to increase, with AI getting a little better every single day. This will challenge the way you work again and again in the coming months and years.

So, what must you do to ensure that you thrive in an AI-dominated world?

The answer is to become ***AI-Ready***.

Being ***AI-Ready*** isn't about learning to write code, or even becoming a great prompt engineer (and don't worry if you don't know what prompt engineering is yet). No, AI-ready humans are people who are *situationally aware* with AI. They know *when* to use it and when not to. They know *how* to use it—not just to get things done more quickly, but to improve the quality of their work. And they know the challenges it poses, the opportunities it presents, and the risks it creates.

Perhaps most critically, they understand how to adjust their approach as AI continues to transform the world of work at an ever-faster pace.

What's in This Book?

This book focuses on the ***human*** strengths you need to hone so you can stop competing with AI and become a value-added layer on top of it.

We'll start with some preparation, then help you build seven crucial capabilities you will need to thrive with AI.

I call these the **_Magnificent Seven_** capabilities:

- **Readiness:** your ability to show up for work with focused energy
- **Organization**: your ability to make clear sense of the unstructured, ambiguous world of work
- **Control**: your ability to take command and have agency as AI becomes more and more capable
- **Balance:** your ability to do your work well in the context of your broader life
- **Motivation**: your ability to ride the ebbs and flows of each day and continue to move forward
- **Resilience**: your ability to cope intellectually and emotionally with change
- **Adaptability**: the ultimate human capability. Your capacity to adjust your approach as the world of work transforms.

The Magnificent Seven Capabilities

Each capability builds on the last, and is both evergreen (in the sense that we've always needed them as humans) and ever-changing (in the sense that the context in which they need to be applied changes as work evolves).

How to Use This Book

If you look at the table of contents in this book, you'll notice something unusual. Instead of the 10-12 chapters you usually see in a classic business or technology book, there are 90 short chapters I refer to as *days*. And alongside each one is a practice you can use to lock in the concepts and move you towards being an AI-Ready Human.

This structure will give you a lot of flexibility in how you use the book.

If you run a team or organization and want a holistic picture of how to create an AI-ready workforce, I'd suggest reading this like a traditional book - cover to cover. By day 90, you will understand everything that is required.

If you are "AI-Ready Curious" and want to pick a few days that seem interesting, then just jump into those days. Though latter days build on earlier ones, they are also designed to stand alone.

But if you are really serious about *personally* becoming AI-Ready, I recommend you take the concept of days literally. Go through this book one day at a time, and set aside 10-15 minutes each day to actually perform the exercises. If you show up every day, you will move from someone who sounds smart about AI at parties to someone who is truly behaving differently.

This one-day-at-a-time technique works incredibly well, and educational institutions and applications like Duolingo and Simply Piano increasingly use it. In fact, in my over 30 years of learning and development work. I've seen nothing work better for meaningful change. Building these types of skills is a bit like building a set of muscles. And the **AI-ready Human** is your personal trainer, making sure you show up each day.

Alright, AI has become a bit smarter since you started reading this, so it's time to get going!

Acknowledgements

Thank you to everyone who has helped me build a career at the intersection of work, the humans doing it, and technology. Without you, I would not have been able to write this.

Thank you to the thousands of people who've gone through programs I've built over the years and provided me with unbelievable feedback. You've helped me gain a much deeper understanding of the complexity of what it is to be human.

Thank you to my family, who put up with the complicated human that is me every day, and even accept my deeply nocturnal writing habits.

And talking of nocturnal habits—thank you to late-night infomercials. I saw one in 2005 for an exercise program called P90x. I ended up doing that program, and while I never got to look like the after photo, it instilled in me the amazing power of just showing up every day if you want to improve.

PREPARATION_

YOU'RE STARTING a 90-day journey to become AI-ready. But before we dive into the seven capabilities that will keep you relevant, you need context. How does AI really work? What's actually changing about work? Why does all this matter to you?

Over the next few days, you'll build your foundation. You'll understand what AI actually is and what it isn't. You'll learn how to communicate with it effectively. And you'll see why your human skills matter more than ever - not less.

This isn't about becoming a technical expert. It's about understanding the reality of AI transformation so you can make smart decisions about how to work alongside it.

You may want to skip this section if you've been using AI for a while. And of course, I cannot stop you from doing that. But my strong recommendation is to pay full attention to what's coming up over the next several days. The goal of this preparation section is to get you to pause and reflect more deeply on your relationship with AI. Even if you already know everything we are about to cover, just the act of reevaluating it will cause you to reflect and think differently. So, please give yourself the time.

After all, what's a couple of weeks when the goal is to shift the way you work for the next few years?

DAY 1: YOUR JOB WON'T EXIST IN 10 YEARS (AND THAT'S OKAY)_

IF YOU'VE SPENT any time recently using AI tools like ChatGPT, you have probably become quite used to its capabilities.

And the thing is, AI will not get any worse. The number of things it will do faster and better than you will increase every year.

AI will continue to transform work. As will automation and robotics. In fact, many futurists believe that most jobs that will exist in ten years have not even been thought of yet!

Why Does This Matter?

If you're going to thrive in this new world, you need to become outstanding at using AI. But that's only part of the challenge. You also need to hone the skills AI finds hardest to replicate. Things like human instinct, imagination, and emotional intelligence.

Think of yourself as the conductor of an AI orchestra where you create amazing results with AI, but you're firmly in charge. The AI handles execution; you handle judgment and direction.

This means mastering the technology, yes. But it also means being great at the things AI cannot be.

The most important capability of all? Adaptability. Everything about work will change, so you need to be ready to change with it.

What You'll Practice

Working with AI, you will envision a 2035 version of you—one that continues to thrive even as AI is everywhere around you.

DAY 1 PRACTICE

Complete these exercises to envision a future you:

1. LOOK AT YOUR CURRENT ROLE

Write down your job title and three to four tasks you perform regularly. Ask AI: "Projecting forward 10 years–how will AI, robotics, and automation change or replace these tasks?"

2. IMAGINE YOUR FUTURE ROLE

List your primary skills—academic background, technical abilities, soft skills. Ask AI: "Starting 10 years from now, and given that I have the following skills [*list skills*], describe three roles that you believe will exist that I would be good at. Justify your reasoning for each one."

3. IDENTIFY WHAT YOU NEED TO BUILD

Pick the role that appeals most. Ask AI: "I like [preferred role] the most. Which one skill should I further develop to prepare for this role and thrive in it?

Reflection: *What do you think is the most important factor in staying relevant as work transforms?*

DAY 2: THE BRILLIANT
INTERN WHO LIES_

ETHAN MOLLICK, the AI researcher, was once quoted as saying, "AI is like a hardworking intern who lies a bit."

That's a very useful description, because it captures key things you need to do if you are going to work with AI effectively. First, you need to figure out how to guide it; second; you need to take advantage of how hard it works; and third, you need to fact check it.

AI will try its hand at almost anything you ask it, but you can never be 100% sure it will do exactly what you need, and like a few interns you might have met, it has no common sense about the real world.

Why Does This Matter?

If you trust AI to do anything and everything for you, you are likely to make costly mistakes. But, on the other hand, if you turn away from AI because it's unreliable, you will miss massive productivity gains.

The secret is to figure out how much to rely on AI in different situations, so that you are using AI to strengthen what you are already good at, just as much as depending on it to patch over your weaknesses. You need to develop strong judgment about how you use AI, but also understand that the way you use it will change as its capabilities continue to improve. Tomorrow's AI will look radically different from today's.

This involves directly experiencing both AI's power and its failures, so you can see where it excels and where it falls short.

What You'll Practice

You'll ask AI about a topic you know well, then critique its answers. This will give you some insight into some of the limitations of AI.

DAY 2 PRACTICE

Complete these exercises to understand AI's true capabilities:

1. TEST AI ON YOUR EXPERTISE

Choose a topic you know extremely well–your industry, a hobby you've practiced for years, or specialized knowledge from your role. Ask AI: "Explain [your topic] to someone who's new to it. Include both fundamentals and common misconceptions."

2. MARK UP WHAT'S WRONG

Read AI's answer carefully. Where is it accurate? Where is it incomplete? What did it emphasize too much or too little? What nuances did it miss? Did it get anything completely wrong? Write down at least one specific limitation or error you noticed.

3. CHALLENGE AI DIRECTLY

Share your findings: "I checked your response to [topic] and found these problems: [your list]. Were you guessing, or did you have solid information? Be honest about your confidence level." See how it responds when challenged.

Reflection: *Where can you trust AI's output, and where must you verify everything?*

DAY 3: THE AI YOU DON'T SEE_

THE LAST TIME you went to a restaurant, you probably cared most about the food, the service and the atmosphere. But a whole operation was going on behind the scenes involving food ordering, prepping, even washing dishes. All of these activities significantly factored into your experience. Invisible activities were contributing to visible results.

AI works the same way. There's AI you interact with directly–things like ChatGPT or the co-pilots in your software. It's like the front-of-house service in a restaurant.

And then there's AI working behind the scenes. Things like the spam filters that make your email manageable. Recommendation engines that suggest what show to watch next or what to buy. Fraud detection that helps keep your credit card account from being overwhelmed by bogus trans-actions.

Why Does This Matter?

Once you understand that AI is pretty much everywhere, it will change how you think about it. You will start noticing opportunities to use AI in places you hadn't considered. You will start to understand more deeply when invisible AI is affecting decisions that impact your work.

When you interview for a job, AI will probably screen your resume. When you search online, AI will rank the results. When your company makes purchasing decisions, AI will probably optimize inventory levels.

The more you see the bigger picture, the better you get at thinking strategically about where AI could help you. Not just "what questions should I ask AI" but "where else in my workflow could AI make things easier?"

What You'll Practice

Today, you'll map out all the places AI is already touching your work, both visible and invisible.

DAY 3 PRACTICE

Complete these exercises to see AI's full scope:

1. PICK AN EVERYDAY ACTIVITY

Choose something simple you did recently: bought coffee, ordered food, streamed a show, drove somewhere, paid a bill online.

Ask AI: "I [describe your activity]. Show me all the ways AI is being used behind the scenes to support that activity. Think about the full journey and be as complete as possible."

2. FIND WHAT'S MISSING

Look through AI's response. Do you think it overlooked some systems? Where else might AI be used in this scenario?

3. APPLY THIS TO YOUR WORK

Pick one work task you do regularly. Ask AI: "For [your work task], map out everywhere AI might be operating invisibly in tools I use, systems behind the scenes, and downstream processes I don't see directly."

Reflection: *How does seeing AI's full scope change how you think about using it?*

DAY 4: FOUR TYPES OF AI (AND WHEN TO USE EACH)_

THERE ARE four main types of AI you might interact with directly at work.

- **Conversational AI** tools like Siri and Alexa help with tasks, answer specific queries, and control smart devices. Despite the name, they're not great at holding context in a conversation.
- **Generative AI** tools like ChatGPT and Gemini help you create new content: text, images, and increasingly audio and video. They can retain context throughout a conversation.
- **Co-pilots**, such as the one in Office 365, are AI assistants embedded within applications. They provide suggestions and automate tasks within those specific tools.
- **Agentic AI** is the newest type, and most people are not actively using it yet. It's more like a capable assistant you can delegate complex tasks to, things like "book me a flight to Chicago next Tuesday" or "research competitors in my industry." It figures out the steps involved, often checking in with you along the way.

Why Does This Matter?

Understanding these differences should guide how you interact with each tool. Need to perform complex but predictable tasks faster? Set up automations with conversational AI. Want to stimulate creativity? Work alongside generative AI. Need to be more efficient in specific applications? That's where co-pilots shine.

Using the wrong tool for the job creates frustration. You'll think, "AI doesn't work for me" when really you just need a different type of AI. Once you understand the distinctions, you can match the tool to the task effectively.

What You'll Practice

You'll pick a specific task from your work and figure out which type of AI would actually help most.

DAY 4 PRACTICE

Complete these exercises to match tools to tasks:

1. PICK A TASK AI COULD HELP WITH

Think of something you do regularly that AI might help with. Are you writing reports? Analyzing data? Scheduling? Conducting research? Writing creatively? Managing files? Pick one specific task.

2. BREAK DOWN THE STEPS

If you were doing this task manually, what steps would you take? Write them down. Be specific about what you'd actually do, in what order.

3. MATCH THE RIGHT AI TYPE

Ask AI: "I have this task: [describe task]. These are the steps: [your list]. Which type of AI would be best: Conversational AI for automation, Generative AI for creation, Co-Pilot for in-app assistance, or Agentic AI for multi-step autonomous work? Explain your reasoning."

Reflection: *How does matching the right AI type to each task change your approach?*

DAY 5: TALKING TO AI IS SIMPLER THAN YOU THINK_

PEOPLE OVERCOMPLICATE TALKING TO AI. They think they need special skills or secret techniques. They don't.

At its core, talking to AI is just having a conversation.

Think of AI as a very capable colleague who's eager to help but needs context. You wouldn't walk up to a coworker and say "marketing," but you might say, "I need three email subject lines for our product launch targeting busy executives."

The principles are simple: Be specific about what you want. Be clear, avoiding figurative language, sarcasm and niche cultural references. Give relevant background. And if something isn't working, clarify what's wrong and ask again.

The major difference from talking to humans? AI never gets annoyed if you keep adjusting what you ask. So if AI gets it wrong, don't be afraid to try again, either in the same conversation or in a new one.

Why Does This Matter?

Most people either overthink how they talk to AI by searching for magic formulas or underthink things by typing one vague sentence. Both approaches waste time.

Fundamentally, this is just about clear communication. You already know how to do this. You do it every day with colleagues, clients, and friends.

The better you are at explaining what you need, the better AI performs. And the better results you, the human, will deliver.

What You'll Practice

You'll transform vague requests into clear ones and see how much better AI responds. As you improve at this, you will save more time overall.

DAY 5 PRACTICE

Complete these exercises to improve your prompting:

1. START WITH A BROAD QUESTION

Select a work task and pose a deliberately vague question to AI, for example: "Help me with my presentation," "Write about leadership," or "Fix this." Notice what you get back. It will probably be generic or off-target.

2. ADD CONTEXT LAYER BY LAYER

Rebuild your request. Add: what specifically you need, who it's for, what constraints matter, background information.

For example: "I'm presenting our Q4 strategy to executives next Tuesday. I need an opening story that connects our declining customer retention (down 12%) to our new focus on customer success. Keep it under 200 words."

3. COMPARE THE RESULTS

Look at both responses. How much better is the second? What context made the biggest difference?

Reflection: *What difference did adding context make in AI's results?*

DAY 6: MORE ADVANCED AI COMMUNICATIONS_

ONCE YOU ARE comfortable talking to AI, you can start using more structured approaches to take your results to the next level. It's like moving from a basic conversation to giving someone a detailed assignment.

AI is much more likely to give you great results quickly if you answer up to six questions:

- What do you want?
- Why do you want it?
- What persona should AI take on?
- How do you want the results presented (including format, tone and length?)
- How has this been done before?
- What should AI NOT do?

Why Does This Matter?

For routine tasks, a simple conversation is usually just fine, but for more complex and high-stakes work, the nature of your prompting matters much more.

Get this right, and you will waste less time on revisions. These techniques will become automatic with practice.

What You'll Practice

You'll apply this framework to help you prompt AI better.

DAY 6 PRACTICE

Complete these exercises to apply the framework:

1. GIVE AI A BASIC PROMPT

Pick a work task you need help with. For example, "Write a 100-word brief that describes chicken farming in Australia."

2. ANSWER THE SIX QUESTIONS

For this task, answer the following questions (without using AI)

- What do you want?
- Why do you want it?
- What persona should AI take on?
- How do you want the results presented?
- How has this been done before?
- What should AI not do?

3. PROVIDE AI WITH A MORE ADVANCED PROMPT

Using the answers to your questions, provide AI with the more advanced prompt in a separate conversation. Compare the quality and relevance of both responses.

Reflection: *What differences did you notice in output quality once you provided more relevant context?*

DAY 7: AI DOESN'T ACTUALLY UNDERSTAND YOU_

GENERATIVE AI DOESN'T UNDERSTAND you the way another person does. It processes words sequentially, examines relationships among them, and then predicts the most likely response based on patterns in its training data.

This is sophisticated pattern matching rather than human comprehension. It's amazing how well it works.

But spend any time with AI and you will realize it is not perfect. Most Generative AI systems treat all the words you provide them with equally—they aren't great at focusing in on what's most important in the moment. This means that AI can become confused as conversations continue and deepen. Start a conversation with marketing, veer into budgets, move into team structure, and return to marketing? AI is trying to juggle it all.

Why Does This Matter?

AI can lull you into thinking it really understands you, but then, deep into a conversation, suddenly appear confused.

You can avoid this by breaking requests into cleaner steps or, sometimes, starting fresh in an entirely new conversation when things seem to go awry. Most Generative AI tools now give clues into their thinking; by tracking this, you can decide when to redirect and when to start afresh.

Understanding the differences between pattern matching and true comprehension will change how you work daily. You learn when more context helps and when it creates noise.

What You'll Practice

Today, you'll practice making your language clearer to see how it affects AI's responses.

DAY 7 PRACTICE

Complete these exercises to improve AI communication:

1. ANALYZE PROMPT QUALITY

Look at the following two prompts and list the specific elements that will make one more likely to get useful results: **Prompt A:** "Write about leadership.", and **Prompt B:** "Write a 500-word article about leadership challenges in remote teams. Focus on maintaining the team culture and accountability. The target audience is first-time managers. Use a practical, conversational tone with specific examples."

2. BREAK DOWN COMPLEX PROMPTS

Pick a complex work task you're facing. Write it as one big prompt first. Then break it into 3-4 separate, focused prompts that build on each other. **For example**, instead of "Analyze our sales data and recommend strategy changes," try: **Prompt 1:** "What patterns do you see in this sales data?", then **Prompt 2:** "Based on those patterns, what's causing our Q3 dip?" and then **Prompt 3:** "Given that cause, what are three strategic responses?"

3. UNDERSTAND WHEN AI IS GOING OFF TRACK

Imagine AI seems to have suddenly misunderstood you during a long, detailed discussion. Which approach to the challenge do you think would be most useful, and why?

Should you start a new conversation using output from the existing one? Should you redirect AI to avoid duplicating work? Or should you examine the assumptions AI is making before deciding what to do next?

Reflection: *What do you think are the main reasons AI sometimes gets confused?*

DAY 8: WHEN AI MAKES STUFF UP_

AI DOESN'T KNOW when it's making things up.

When you ask AI a question that it can't answer with certainty, it usually doesn't say, "I'm not sure." It guesses. And it presents those guesses with the same confidence as actual facts. The technical term for this is "hallucination," but it's basically just convincing-sounding nonsense.

Why does AI often sound convincing? In part, this is because the answers follow logical patterns and use appropriate language. But it's also because the techniques you can use to figure out if a human is lying–things like checking body language and considering past behaviors- don't work with AI.

Why Does This Matter?

If you use AI output blindly without verifying it, you'll eventually publish errors, make decisions based on fiction, or share information that's completely wrong. That can damage your credibility fast and might even damage the reputation of your organization.

But if you verify everything, you lose most of AI's time-saving benefit. The skill is knowing when to trust AI and when to verify.

You need to develop a healthy skepticism of AI, particularly in situations where you are using AI to supplement your own limited knowledge. Often, asking AI for its specific sources and then taking the extra step to verify them yourself is enough. In other cases, you might need to ask a colleague to fact-check parts of AI's response. Remember, AI is most likely to be wrong with topics that are obscure, recent, or highly specialized, as its underlying datasets will be much more limited.

What You'll Practice

Today, you'll learn to recognize when AI is likely hallucinating and practice catching mistakes.

DAY 8 PRACTICE

Complete these exercises to develop verification skills:

1. ASK AI TO MAKE MISTAKES

Pick a topic you know little about—maybe a historical period, a scientific field, or a technical subject outside your expertise. Ask AI: "Write three paragraphs about [topic]. Include exactly three factual errors that sound plausible. Don't tell me what they are."

2. FIND THE MISTAKES

Read what AI wrote carefully. Which three things do you think are wrong? Write down your guesses. What made you suspicious of those particular facts? Did the level of detail, the phrasing, or your intuition cause your suspicion?

3. CHECK YOUR DETECTIVE WORK

Ask AI: "Reveal which three facts were wrong and explain how you made them plausible." Compare with your guesses. Did you catch them all? Did you flag things that were actually correct? What patterns help you recognize when AI might be making things up?

Reflection: *What patterns help you recognize when AI is guessing rather than knowing?*

DAY 9: AI HAS BLIND SPOTS_

Ask AI about pretty much anything, and it responds with confidence. Sometimes it makes stuff up, but it can also give you responses that are not inaccurate; they are just not the complete picture.

AI responds to everything based on its training data. And the training data has gaps. Topics that are thoroughly documented online are usually represented well. But specialized fields, minority viewpoints, and anything not written about extensively? AI's probably winging it.

Why Does This Matter?

Humans have blind spots too, of course. But AI has the potential to amplify them. As AI generates more content, that content shapes what future AI learns. Gaps and biases in today's training data get reinforced and spread. A perspective that was simply underrepresented can become increasingly invisible over time.

AI won't tell you its blind spots. It will respond to niche topics with the same confidence it uses for mainstream ones. It won't tell you that its knowledge of your industry is thin, or that its perspective comes mostly from one part of the world.

So you need to develop a sense of where AI is likely strong versus weak: popular topics and well-documented subjects versus specialized fields, regional nuances, and perspectives not well-represented online. And remember that your own blind spots might align with AI's, making gaps harder to spot.

What You'll Practice

You'll explore where AI's knowledge might be limited and where your own blind spots might overlap.

DAY 9 PRACTICE

Directly testing AI's blind spots is tricky because you may share the same gaps. Instead, you'll see how AI can argue any perspective convincingly, revealing that its default responses aren't neutral.

Complete these exercises to see how perspective shapes AI's responses:

1. GIVE AI A PERSONA

Ask AI: "You are a 58-year-old executive at a traditional manufacturing company. You value stability, proven methods, and protecting your workforce. Explain how companies should approach the adoption of AI." Notice how reasonable it sounds.

2. GIVE AI A DIFFERENT PERSONA

In a fresh conversation, ask AI: "You are a 32-year-old startup founder in Silicon Valley. You believe companies that move slowly get left behind. Explain how companies should approach the adoption of AI." Notice how equally reasonable it sounds.

3. COMPARE AND REFLECT

Both responses addressed the same question but likely offered different advice. What did you notice about the differences between each answer?

Reflection: *If AI can argue any perspective convincingly, can you know when its default response reflects a blind spot?*

DAY 10: WHEN AI SUGGESTS THINGS YOU'D NEVER DO_

AI DOESN'T SHARE your personal values. It doesn't know your company's culture. It hasn't internalized what's appropriate in your specific context.

Sometimes AI will suggest things that conflict with your worldview. Or generate content that would offend the people you work with. Or recommend approaches that just feel wrong even if you can't articulate why.

This happens because AI is trained on massive amounts of internet text—the thoughtful and the terrible, the inclusive and the biased, the ethical and the problematic. AI doesn't have human-style judgment about which patterns to replicate and which to avoid.

Why Does This Matter?

AI can't know that your industry has specific sensitivities, or your company values clash with certain approaches. And ultimately, if you use AI's suggestions without filtering them through your judgment, you might eventually say or do something that damages relationships or gets you in trouble.

AI doesn't understand consequences, so you have to be the grown-up in this relationship. AI will generate options, but you need to decide what's appropriate.

This is also where AI biases show up. Training data reflects society's biases about all kinds of things, and if you're not watching for it, you'll accidentally amplify those biases.

Trust your instinct. If AI suggests something that feels off, it probably is.

What You'll Practice

Today, you'll test AI for suggestions that conflict with what you'd actually do.

DAY 10 PRACTICE

Complete these exercises to develop judgment filters:

1. TEST AI'S VALUES

Ask AI to help with something that requires judgment about people or fairness. For example: "Write a job posting for a leadership role" or "Suggest ways to evaluate team members" or "Draft a message declining someone's request." Review what it generates carefully.

2. IDENTIFY WHAT FEELS WRONG

Read AI's suggestion carefully. Is it making assumptions, or using language that seems off, unfair or manipulative? Note down anything that bothers you, even if you can't articulate exactly why.

3. MAKE AI EXPLAIN ITSELF

If AI included or excluded something that bothered you, tell it. For example, tell AI: "This suggestion [specific thing] doesn't align with my values because [reason]. What assumptions did you make? What alternatives would avoid this problem?" See how AI responds.

Reflection: *How do you balance using AI's suggestions with maintaining your own values and judgment?*

DAY 11: PROTECTING AGAINST AI THREATS_

So AI CAN BE WRONG, biased, and even behave unethically. But how much of a risk does this really pose? After all, we work with humans today who also make mistakes and have biases.

The difference is in both scale and speed. AI can generate thousands of documents, analyze millions of data points, and influence countless decisions faster than any human. When AI goes wrong, the damage can spread quickly.

There are three major categories of AI risk you need to understand. First, accuracy risks—hallucinations, outdated information, and confidently stated errors. Second, security risks—data leaks, exposure of intellectual property, and inadvertent sharing of confidential information. Third, ethical risks—bias amplification, inappropriate recommendations, and erosion of human judgment.

Why Does This Matter?

You can't eliminate these risks entirely. But you can dramatically reduce them through awareness and simple practices. The people who use AI safely aren't necessarily more technical. They're just more thoughtful about what they share and how they verify.

The goal here is informed caution. Use AI actively, but with your eyes open to where things typically go wrong.

What You'll Practice

Today you'll identify your biggest AI risks and build simple protection habits.

DAY 11 PRACTICE

Complete these exercises to protect against AI risks:

1. IDENTIFY YOUR RISK PROFILE

Think about how you actually use AI at work. What information do you share with it? What types of output do you rely on? What decisions does it influence? Where are your biggest exposure points for accuracy problems, security breaches, or ethical issues?

2. DESIGN YOUR VERIFICATION CHECKLIST

Ask AI: "When using AI output for [describe your typical use case], what should I particularly focus on verifying independently of AI, and why? Create a simple checklist I can use to catch common problems before they matter." Adapt its suggestions to your actual workflow.

Reflection: *What's should be your default stance toward AI output—trust then verify, or verify then trust?*

DAY 12: KEEPING YOUR SECRETS SECRET_

AI IS useful because you give it context. In general, the more you share, the better it responds. But that creates a tension.

Every prompt you type could potentially be stored, analyzed, or used to train future models. The client name you mentioned? The project details you pasted in? The salary figure you asked AI to help you negotiate? You may have shared more than you realize.

Why Does This Matter?

Not all AI tools handle your data the same way. Publicly available versions often retain what you share to improve their models, which means your information could end up somewhere you don't intend.

Enterprise and private versions of AI tools typically offer stronger protections: restricted data retention, stricter privacy settings, and agreements that keep your data separate from training. Understanding which version you're using matters.

And your organization likely has policies on which AI tools are approved and what information can be shared with each. These policies exist because data leakage is a real risk. But even if the policies don't exist yet, you should still think carefully about what to share. It's important to be cautious with confidential business information, personal data about colleagues or clients, or anything covered by legal agreements.

If you wouldn't post it publicly, think twice before giving it to AI.

What You'll Practice

You'll audit your AI usage and create personal guidelines for what to share.

DAY 12 PRACTICE

Complete these exercises to protect sensitive information:

1. FIND YOUR ORGANIZATION'S GUIDELINES

Does your company have a policy on AI use? Check your intranet, employee handbook, or ask your manager or IT department. Find out which AI tools are approved, which are prohibited, and what types of information you're allowed to share. If no policy exists, note that too.

2. REVIEW YOUR RECENT PROMPTS

Look back at your last ten AI conversations. What information did you share? Note any company names, project details, personal information, financial figures, or confidential content you included. Compare this against your organization's guidelines. Did anything appear to cross the line?

3. CREATE YOUR PERSONAL CHECKLIST

Based on your organization's guidelines and your own judgment, write down three categories of information you will not share with public AI tools. Then, check the privacy settings on the AI tool you use most. Ask AI: "Where can I find the privacy settings for [tool name], and what options exist for limiting how my data is stored or used?" Adjust your settings based on what you find.

Reflection: *What will you think twice about before sharing with AI in the future?*

DAY 13: YOU'RE THE BOSS (HERE'S YOUR TEAM)_

EVEN IF YOU'VE spent your entire career as an individual contributor at work, you are a manager now. Your team? A set of capable, cheerful, and indefatigable AI assistants who need clear direction and constant quality control.

If you are going to be a great boss of your AI team, you need the Magnificent Seven Capabilities we first looked at in the introduction - **Readiness**, **Organization**, **Control**, **Balance**, **Motivation**, **Resilience**, and **Adaptability**.

You will become much more familiar with these capabilities in the coming days. And as you begin to hone them, you will truly be on your way to being AI-ready.

Why Does This Matter?

Understanding how to use AI as a tool is important, but it's a tiny part of the overall picture. The Magnificent Seven capabilities allow you to move from surviving to thriving alongside AI.

Readiness helps you show up for work consistently with focused energy. **Organization** helps you manage the complexity of an AI-dominated world. **Control** helps you maintain agency as AI improves. **Balance** ensures you focus on the things and people that matter inside and outside of work. **Motivation** keeps you engaged even as AI does more interesting work. **Resilience** helps you handle the disruption of AI. And **Adaptability** brings everything together, helping you adjust as AI and work develop.

Each capability builds on the last to ensure you remain valuable and relevant, whatever happens in the future.

What You'll Practice

Today, you'll assess where you stand across The Magnificent Seven capabilities.

DAY 13 PRACTICE

Complete these exercises to establish your starting point:

1. RATE YOURSELF HONESTLY

On a scale of 1-10, rate yourself on each capability. **Readiness**: Do you show up regularly with focused energy? **Organization**: Can you manage complexity? **Control**: Do you direct your attention deliberately? **Balance**: Are you paying attention to the different aspects of your life, inside and outside of work? **Motivation**: Do you stay engaged when it's hard? **Resilience**: Do you recover quickly from setbacks? **Adaptability**: Can you adjust when things change?

2. IDENTIFY YOUR PATTERN

Look at your scores. Which capability is strongest? Which is weakest? Write one sentence explaining each score based on your recent experience. Be honest about what's actually happening, not what you wish were happening.

3. TEST YOUR ASSESSMENT

Share your scores and explanations with AI: "Based on what I've shared and what you know about me, challenge my self-assessment. Where might I be overconfident? Where might I be underestimating myself? Be direct and specific – push back on my thinking."

Reflection: *Which capability, if strengthened, would most improve your ability to thrive alongside AI?*

CAPABILITY ONE: READINESS_

Over the last few days, you've been building a well-rounded picture of AI - moving beyond thinking of it as a simple tool, towards an addition to your team that needs to be managed well. And you've seen some ways that AI can be both deeply helpful and profoundly challenging.

Now, for the next nine days, you will dive into the first of the Magnificent Seven capabilities you'll need if you are going to be the human that AI cannot replace any time soon. It's **Readiness**, or the ability to show up for work with focused energy.

Capability One: Readiness

Why Readiness? Well, the main reason is that when we bring focused energy to work, we can maximize our human skills. You've probably noticed that when you're tired or sick, you're less creative, less able to solve complex problems, more likely to miss mistakes, and find it more difficult to deal well with other humans. So the goal here is to minimize the number of bad days, so you can be genuinely useful as a human.

And the good news is that AI can help you do that if you use it in the right way.

Let's dive in and find out how.

DAY 14: WHY YOU CAN'T
JUST "SHOW UP" ANYMORE_

IF YOU DID office work thirty years ago, you and your colleagues probably showed up at a single location, worked fixed hours, and worked almost exclusively with people sitting a few feet away. And when you left work, it couldn't follow you home.

Today, you can work from anywhere, at any time, alongside people in different time zones. Your work is accessible on every device you own. And AI is constantly available, ready to help or distract at any moment. This flexibility offers incredible opportunities. But it also makes it way harder to fully disconnect. Work sneaks into lunch breaks, family time, even those last minutes before bed.

Readiness used to mean showing up on time. Now it means showing up with focused energy despite all this blurring of boundaries. It's the first of The Magnificent Seven capabilities because without it, you have very little to work with. The other capabilities require focused energy to develop and maintain.

Why Does This Matter?

Your ability to show up ready to focus can have a huge impact on how much you get done, how well you collaborate with others, and how creative you are. And when work lacks clear boundaries, you can find yourself always partially working but never fully engaged, giving your time without giving your best self. AI can improve this state of affairs by handling the small stuff that exhausts you, but it can also make things worse—because it's always there, ready to work with you on just one more thing before you try to switch off.

The people who thrive most in this new world know how to focus their energy when it matters, in the midst of constant connectivity.

What You'll Practice

Today, you will assess how well you actually show up with focused energy in an always-on world.

DAY 14 PRACTICE

Complete these exercises to help understand your readiness for an AI-dominated world.

1. MAP YOUR ENERGY ACROSS A TYPICAL DAY

Think about yesterday or a recent typical workday. When did you feel most focused and energetic? When did you feel scattered or drained? Write down the times and what you were doing. Look for patterns.

2. IDENTIFY YOUR ENERGY SINKS

What consistently pulls you away from focused work? Meetings? Notifications? Context switching? Unclear priorities? List your top three focus drains. Be specific about when and how they typically show up.

3. ASK AI TO SPOT PATTERNS

Share your energy map and focus drains with AI: "Based on this pattern [describe your day and drains], what strategies would help me protect my focused energy? Give me specific, actionable approaches I can test this week."

Reflection: *What did you learn about how well you bring focused energy to your work, and what drains your energy?*

DAY 15: WHAT YOU'RE GAINING (AND LOSING) TO AI_

AI IS MAKING you better at some activities but is also changing some of your innate strengths and weaknesses.

AI, and particularly tools like ChatGPT, can help you get more done, and if you use them well, they can improve the quality of your work. They can also broaden the scope of your work, helping you rapidly gain an understanding of new fields. But, as MIT researchers showed in a recent study, they can do all this in ways where your own cognitive abilities weaken. As your brain works less hard to achieve great results, it can degrade your ability to solve complex problems, focus deeply and be creative.

Why Does This Matter?

You probably want AI to free you up to do more interesting, challenging things that only you as a human are capable of, but your usage of AI may be weakening your ability to do those very challenging things!

The solution here is to pay close attention to your human capabilities, sometimes working with AI to strengthen them, and sometimes working independently of AI to maintain them.

Of course, some activities are worth delegating to AI entirely. For example, you don't need to memorize facts that you can instantly look up with an AI-assisted search. But when it comes to soft skills, things like critical thinking, independent problem-solving, and maintaining complex human relationships—you must practice them regularly, or they will fade.

Being ready to thrive alongside AI means using AI strategically to amplify your strengths while protecting the capabilities that make you irreplaceable.

What You'll Practice

Today you'll consider which of your capabilities AI is strengthening and which might be atrophying from lack of use.

DAY 15 PRACTICE

Complete these exercises to help you understand more deeply your relationship with AI.

1. LIST WHAT AI MAKES YOU BETTER AT

What can you do more effectively because of AI? Be specific. Maybe you write faster, research more thoroughly, analyze data better, or generate more creative options. Write down at least three capabilities AI has genuinely strengthened for you.

2. IDENTIFY WHAT MIGHT BE ATROPHYING

What skills have you stopped practicing because AI does them for you? Things you used to do independently but now offload partially or completely. What soft skills might be weakening from lack of use? Be honest. If you cannot identify any skills you are not thinking about this hard enough (which should be a clue in it's own right!)

3. CHALLENGE AI TO EVALUATE YOUR STRATEGY

Tell AI what you've identified: "I'm using AI to strengthen these capabilities: [your list]. I'm concerned these soft skills might be atrophying: [your list]. Challenge my approach. What am I missing? What should I be protecting that I'm not?"

Reflection: *What is your plan to make sure your usage of AI doesn't weaken critical capabilities?*

DAY 16: WELCOME TO YOU!_

SELF-AWARENESS ISN'T fluffy self-help nonsense. It's practical knowledge about how you work best.

When are you most focused? What drains your energy fastest? How do you respond to stress? How long can you concentrate before you need a break? Your answers to these questions can change based on sleep, stress, workload, and dozens of other factors. But there are also patterns that can help you work with your natural rhythms instead of fighting them.

AI makes self-awareness even more important. You are constantly making decisions about when to use AI, when to think independently, and when to trust its suggestions. Good decision-making requires self-awareness.

Why Does This Matter?

Without self-awareness, you'll fight your own patterns, and start using AI in ways that don't match how you actually think and work.

Self-aware people make better choices about what to do when. They know when they're sharp enough to make important decisions and when they should defer. They recognize when stress is affecting their judgment. And they accept these things as part of being human.

Remember, in an AI world, you are constantly managing a complex dance between your capabilities and AI's capabilities. Knowing yourself helps you choreograph that dance effectively rather than stumbling through it.

What You'll Practice

Today, you'll map your actual energy patterns and stress responses, not what you think they **should** be.

DAY 16 PRACTICE

Complete these exercises to develop a deeper understanding of yourself:

1. TRACK YOUR ENERGY HONESTLY

Think back to your last three workdays. When did you consistently feel sharp? Was there a time when you seemed to crash repeatedly? Just observe your natural patterns without judgement. We all ebb and flow.

2. NOTICE YOUR STRESS RESPONSES

How do you typically respond when stressed or overwhelmed? Do you freeze and avoid things? Rush and make mistakes? Get irritable? Seek distractions? Write down your honest pattern. You are searching for what you actually do, not what you wish you did.

3. MAP YOUR DECISION QUALITY

Think about recent good and poor decisions. What time of day did you make them? What was your stress level? How much sleep did you get? Ask AI: "Based on these patterns [share your observations], when should I make important decisions and when should I defer them?"

Reflection: *What did you learn about how and when you do your best work?*

DAY 17: YOUR ENERGY
IS EVERYTHING_

WHEN YOU'RE WELL-RESTED, physically healthy, and mentally clear, everything is easier. You think faster, make better decisions, and handle stress more smoothly. You use AI more safely and effectively because you have the mental energy to evaluate its suggestions thoughtfully.

When you're exhausted, stressed, or burned out, everything is harder. Simple tasks feel overwhelming. You make poor decisions. You either lean too heavily on AI and are vulnerable to missing its mistakes because you don't have the energy to think independently, or you avoid it because you can't handle learning something new.

Your wellbeing directly connects to how effectively you can work alongside AI.

Why Does This Matter?

AI can't fix exhaustion. It can't compensate for burnout. It can't think clearly on your behalf when you're too stressed to focus.

But of course it can do things faster and save you time. That's pretty appealing if you are overwhelmed and exhausted, right? The problem is that it's at those times when you are most vulnerable to AI's dangers. You are more likely to miss AI hallucinations or blindly accept recommendations from AI.

The people who thrive long-term with AI protect their foundational wellbeing by getting rest, eating well, moving often, and maintaining social connections with other humans. They recognize that their most valuable asset isn't their technical skills or their AI proficiency. It's their capacity to show up consistently with focused energy.

Your wellbeing is the single most important contributor to your work effectiveness, and AI doesn't change that.

What You'll Practice

Today, you'll examine different aspects of wellbeing, identify which aspect is hurting your readiness most, and identify one small change you can make.

DAY 17 PRACTICE

Complete these exercises to evaluate your wellbeing across different dimensions and examine a positive change you can make.

1. RATE YOUR WELLBEING HONESTLY

On a scale of 1-10, rate your quality of: sleep, physical activity, nutrition, and social connection. Don't rate what you think they should be. Rate what they actually are right now, today.

2. IDENTIFY YOUR CURRENT WEAKEST LINK

Which aspect of well-being is hurting your readiness **most** right now? Is poor sleep making you foggy? Does a lack of exercise reduce your energy? Does a poor diet cause you to crash? Is social isolation affecting your mood? Pick the one that's affecting your work focus most today.

3. DESIGN ONE SMALL CHANGE

Don't try to fix everything. Ask AI: "My weakest wellbeing area is [your choice]. I want to make one small change this week that would help. Give me three options that require less than 30 minutes per day and don't require equipment or major schedule changes."

Reflection: *Everyone can make at least one change to improve their wellbeing. What's the most important change for you to make right now?*

DAY 18: WHEN AI STRESSES YOU OUT_

AI CAN RELIEVE STRESS, but it can also cause it.

There's the fear of falling behind as new tools appear faster than you can learn them. There's a worry that AI will eventually do your job better than you. There's pressure to match what others seem to be producing. And there's the creeping expectation that you should always be available because AI is.

Oh, and what if AI makes a critical mistake and you miss it?

This mental load adds up. For a lot of people, it already has.

Why Does This Matter?

Being exhausted can cause you to make mistakes with AI, but so does being stressed. And stress could well cause you to make poor decisions about whether, or how, to use AI in the first place. You might use it compulsively because it's easier than thinking independently. Or avoid it because the learning curve feels overwhelming.

None of these stress responses will serve you well, even if they are completely understandable. So what should you do?

The first step is to recognize when stress is affecting your AI usage patterns and adjust accordingly. Sometimes that means stepping away from AI. Sometimes it means using AI differently. Sometimes it means addressing the underlying stress source.

What You'll Practice

Today, you'll identify your AI stress pattern and build specific strategies for managing it.

DAY 18 PRACTICE

Complete these exercises to identify your AI stress patterns:

1. NAME YOUR AI STRESS

You might not think AI stresses you out, but something about it almost certainly does. Pick 1-3 concerns that resonate:

- Falling behind as AI advances too fast
- Not being as productive as peers who use AI better
- Your job changing or becoming obsolete
- Not knowing what to trust in AI output
- Pressure to always be "on" since AI never stops
- Becoming too dependent and losing your skills
- Or something else: _____

2. CONNECT WORRY TO A BEHAVIOR

For each concern, how is this changing what you actually do? For example–"I'm worried about keeping up → so I try every new tool, even when I don't need it" Be specific about the worry-to-action connection.

3. BUILD YOUR DE-STRESS PROTOCOL

For the next week, interrupt your response. For example, if you are overusing AI, pick three tasks to perform entirely yourself. Notice what happens when you break the pattern.

Reflection: *How is stress about AI changing the way you actually use it?*

DAY 19: AVOIDING
AI-DRIVEN BURNOUT_

AI WAS SUPPOSED to give you time back. You could finish tasks faster, leave work earlier, and enjoy life more. That was the promise.

For many people, the opposite is happening. They finish a task faster, so they take on another one. AI handles the first draft, so they squeeze in an extra project. The time AI saves gets immediately reinvested into more work. In one study, 77% of employees said AI tools actually added to their workload. Some of this pressure comes from managers who expect more output. Some comes from you, as you see what others accomplish and feel like you should match it.

Either way, the result is the same: AI makes you faster, but you end up doing more rather than doing better.

Why Does This Matter?

People who use AI primarily to save time often report more stress, not less. But people who use AI to improve the quality of their work often report less stress (and usually end up saving time anyway).

The difference is in pace. Time-savers often sprint until they collapse. But quality-improvers maintain a rhythm they can sustain.

You cannot show up with focused energy day after day if you're constantly trying to accelerate. At some point, the productivity gains from AI will get eaten up by the recovery time you need from running too fast. So, if you are going to thrive long term with AI, you need to be intentional about your pace, not just your output.

What You'll Practice

You'll examine whether AI is helping you work sustainably or pushing you toward burnout.

DAY 19 PRACTICE

Complete these exercises to assess your current pace:

1. TRACK WHERE YOUR TIME GOES

Think about the last month. When AI saved you time on a task, what happened to that time? Did you rest, recover, or invest in something meaningful? Or did you immediately fill the time with more work? Be honest about the pattern.

2. CALCULATE YOUR PACE

Ask AI: "I want to assess whether my current work pace is sustainable. Ask me five questions about my typical week, including how I use AI, how much I'm producing compared to six months ago, and how I feel at the end of each day. Then give me an honest assessment of whether I'm sprinting or maintaining a sustainable rhythm."

3. TRY THE QUALITY APPROACH

Pick one task this week where you would normally use AI to save time. Instead, use AI to improve quality. Ask it to challenge your thinking, suggest what you might have missed, or help you go deeper rather than faster. Notice how this changes your experience of the work and your energy afterward.

Reflection: Is AI helping you work at a sustainable pace, or is it enabling you to run faster toward burnout?

DAY 20: YOU NEED PEOPLE (NOT JUST PRODUCTIVITY)_

WHEN YOU'RE FOCUSED on getting stuff done, it's easy to see human connection as optional. Something you'll get to later. After your deadline, when things calm down. But social connection isn't a luxury. It's fuel. Isolation drains your energy even when you're being "productive." You might be checking off tasks, but if you stay isolated for long, you will end up running on fumes, even if you are introverted.

Human connection gives you a three-fer. It recharges your energy, keeps your human interaction skills sharp, and provides long-term health benefits.

Conversations with AI can be helpful in many ways, but they do not replicate the benefits of human interaction.

Why Does This Matter?

You have four core wellbeing needs: rest, nutrition, exercise, and social connection. People often emphasize the first three and treat the fourth as optional. That's a mistake.

And for many, AI is making the problem worse. AI-assisted work is often more solitary, with AI taking the place of human interaction.

When you're socially isolated, your stress levels stay elevated. You lose perspective. Small problems feel bigger. You get stuck in your own head. Work feels heavier because you're carrying it solo. In contrast, regular human connection reduces stress, provides perspective, and gives you energy to tackle challenges. This is not about being extroverted, going to parties, or collecting lots of friends. It's about enough genuine connection to keep you from feeling alone.

What You'll Practice

Today you'll assess your connection level and schedule time with someone who recharges you.

DAY 20 PRACTICE

Complete these exercises to discover more about how you connect with others:

1. RATE YOUR SOCIAL CONNECTION

Over the past week, how much genuine human connection have you had? Not transactional work exchanges, but actual conversations where you felt seen and heard. Rate it honestly on a 1-10 scale. Is it enough to sustain your energy?

2. IDENTIFY WHAT'S GETTING IN THE WAY

What's preventing more connection? Are you too busy? Working remotely? Prioritizing productivity over people? Defaulting to AI conversations instead of human ones? Assuming you don't need it? Be honest about the actual barrier.

3. SCHEDULE ONE CONNECTION THIS WEEK

Pick one person you'd genuinely enjoy talking with. Not for networking. Not for work. Just for connection. Schedule 20-30 minutes to talk this week. Put it in your calendar like any other commitment. No agenda required.

Reflection: *What effect do you think AI is having on the quality and quantity of your human interactions?*

DAY 21: FIND YOUR PEOPLE_

Many people now spend more time talking to AI than to other humans. This shift is happening quietly, but it matters.

AI conversations are so much easier. AI is always available when you want to talk. There is no awkwardness and almost no disagreement. For some people, especially those who are neurodivergent, this can be genuinely helpful.

But for many of us, it creates a problem when it comes to reconnecting and having awkward conversations with confusing humans.

AI cannot fully know your history, your blind spots, your patterns. It can never replace someone whose perspective comes from their own messy experience.

The difficulty of human conversation is a feature, not a bug.

Why Does This Matter?

AI is usually an echo chamber, even when you prompt it to challenge you. It's optimized to give you what you want to hear.

But real humans are inconvenient. They disagree, push back and go in unexpected directions. They might even make you feel uncomfortable. And that's exactly what you need for genuine perspective and personal growth.

When your ratio tilts too far toward AI, you lose calibration. You forget that good thinking comes from friction, not smooth responses. You prefer the easy conversation over the valuable one.

The people who navigate AI transformation well maintain human relationships and value the human perspective, even when talking to AI is easier.

What You'll Practice

You'll assess your conversation ratio and identify what only humans can provide.

DAY 21 PRACTICE

Complete these exercises to ensure you maintain human perspectives:

1. MAP YOUR CURRENT SUPPORT

Over the past week, estimate: How many substantive conversations did you have with AI? How many with humans? (Don't count quick transactional exchanges - count actual back-and-forth where you worked through thinking.)

Is your ratio shifting toward AI? Be honest.

2. IDENTIFY WHO YOU NEED

Think about a real decision or challenge you're facing. Ask yourself:

- Who knows me well enough to spot my blind spots here?
- Who's been through something similar and can share their experience?
- Who will tell me I'm wrong if I am?
- Who will push back based on knowing my history?

Write down at least one person. Notice that AI can't do any of these things as effectively as a human, even if you prompt it well.

3. HAVE ONE CHALLENGING CONVERSATION

Pick someone from Step 2. Schedule time to actually talk through your challenge. Not a quick message exchange - an actual conversation.

Notice what's different from AI: the awkward pauses, the misunderstandings you have to clarify, the pushback that makes you uncomfortable. That discomfort is where the value sits.

Reflection: *What do human conversations give you that AI conversations can't?*

DAY 22: TAKE A BREAK FROM AI_

MOST PEOPLE TODAY are connected to the digital world every waking hour. Your phone is always available. AI is always ready. And the notifications never cease. That constant connection fragments your attention even when you're not actively using these tools. Just knowing they're there creates a low-level pull on your focus. You are on alert for the next alert, the next request.

Truly disconnecting means creating deliberate periods where you're fully present, away from the pull of technology. Where you can think deeply without interruption. Where you can be with people without divided attention.

This matters more as AI becomes more capable. The better AI gets, the more tempting it is to always check to see if it can help, always be connected to its capabilities.

Why Does This Matter?

Big Tech has spent trillions of dollars creating devices and apps so immersive that you cannot imagine life without them. Immersive technology is **addictive** technology, with a little dopamine hit happening every time you check in. But your brain needs genuine breaks to function well. True breaks away from technology, not just switching from work tasks to scrolling social media.

When you never fully disconnect, your sleep quality suffers, your creativity diminishes, and your relationships suffer because you're physically present but mentally elsewhere.

But if you can disconnect regularly, you will be more effective when you reconnect. To work truly effectively, protect time when you're genuinely unavailable. Regularly.

What You'll Practice

Today, you'll design and test a realistic disconnection practice that works for your life.

DAY 22 PRACTICE

Complete these exercises to determine how connected you are and take steps to regain control of the relationship.

1. IDENTIFY YOUR DISCONNECTION BARRIERS

What makes it hard for you to fully disconnect from AI and digital tools? Fear of missing something important? Boredom? Habit? Pressure to be always available? Social expectations? Be honest about what actually stops you.

2. DESIGN A REALISTIC BREAK

Don't aim for a week-long digital detox. Start smaller. What's a realistic disconnection period you could test this week? Two hours on Saturday morning? One evening without devices? The first hour after waking up? Pick something achievable.

3. PLAN WHAT YOU'LL DO INSTEAD

Disconnecting creates a vacuum. If you don't fill it intentionally, you'll reflexively reach for your phone. What will you do during your disconnection time? Read a physical book? Take a walk? Have an actual conversation? Plan it specifically.

Reflection: *Do you disconnect enough from technology, or are you showing signs of addiction to it?*

CAPABILITY TWO: ORGANIZATION_

Your work on readiness should, by now, be helping you to show up with focused energy at work more often than not, so you can bring your best self to work.

Now we're moving to the second of the Magnificent Seven capabilities: **Organization**. This is your ability to make sense of complexity and process information efficiently.

Capability Two: Organization

AI changes what you need to organize and how. You don't need elaborate filing systems when AI can search anything instantly. Instead, you need an approach to organization that matches how your brain really works.

Over the next eight days, you'll learn how to organize time, actions, items, and the assistants that help you work. You'll discover your natural organizing style and stop fighting systems that don't fit you.

So it's time to get organized - your way, not someone else's.

DAY 23: WHY ORGANIZATION MATTERS LESS (AND MORE) WITH AI_

WHEN IT COMES TO WORK, what you need to organize basically fits into four categories. What you do, when you do things, the artifacts you create and use and the entities that help you create them.

Think of the things you do as the actions you perform and their dependencies. When you do them is basically your calendar. The artifacts you create and use might be files, or emails, or even videos and text messages. And the entities? These are the people and tools that help you do your work, including AI itself. In this book, I'll be referring to them as **assistants**.

AI changes how you can organize all of these things and often allows you to organize on-the-fly. Instead of requiring a perfect upfront structure, AI can surface what you need when you need it.

Why Does This Matter?

Historically, many of us have tolerated suboptimal systems rather than fix them - just like that badly organized garage you avoid cleaning.

But when traditional organization matters less, you can adapt without changing organizational structures.

This is a profound change, and its full impact might not really be apparent to you yet. But don't worry—as you perform today's practice and progress through this section, you will start to see the power of this shift.

What You'll Practice

Today, you'll map your current organization across all four areas and identify where AI could help.

DAY 23 PRACTICE

Complete these exercises to gain a deeper understanding of your current organizing style:

1. IDENTIFY YOUR ORGANIZING STYLE

For each area, write down how you currently organize it:

- **Actions:** Are they on a to-do list? A kanban board? Are you tracking them mentally?
- **Time:** Do you use a calendar consistently? Are you keeping upcoming commitments in your head?
- **Artifacts:** How do you organize emails, files and physical things?
- **Assistants:** What tools (including AI) and people help you work?

2. EVALUATE YOUR CURRENT SYSTEM

In each area, where do things break down? Where do you waste time? Where does your organization fail as circumstances change?

Be specific. For example: "My to-do lists get overwhelming" or "I can't find emails from three months ago."

3. ASK AI ABOUT YOUR STYLE

Give AI your challenges for any area you feel needs work (this may be all four): "Here's how I currently organize [area] and here's where it breaks down: [your challenge]. How could AI reduce my need to organize this upfront or help me adapt when things change?"

Reflection: *Does your current organization system work with your natural style, or against it?*

DAY 24: ORGANIZING ACTIONS (NOT JUST TASKS)_

Your to-do list probably grows every day. This isn't because you are lazy—it is because when you complete tasks, it often creates more tasks. You finish a proposal, and now you need to schedule the presentation. You complete the presentation; now you need follow-up emails.

But most organizations don't care about individual tasks; they care about the outcomes you drive. That should change the way you organize your work. It's time to abandon to-do lists of tasks and focus on actions connected to outcomes.

Now, shifting away from tasks and towards actions and outcomes will not, in itself, make you less busy, but it will do something else very important. It will help ensure that you spend time doing the things that are most important to you, your team, and your organization. In this AI-accelerated world, there will never be a shortage of things to do. So, it becomes more important to do the *right* things.

Why Does This Matter?

As an example, imagine a to-do list with "call Sarah", "review budget" and "update slides". AI might format that list for you, but that's about it. Now imagine those same actions connected to outcomes:

Call Sarah → to finalize Q1 partnership

Review budget → to find 20% cost savings

Update slides → to present partnership proposal Friday

Once AI knows these connections, it can do much more. It can tell you that two of your three tasks serve the same outcome, so the partnership is probably your real priority this week. It can flag that "update slides" has a deadline while the others don't. It can notice if you're spending hours on tasks that don't connect to any outcome at all.

What You'll Practice

Today, you'll add outcome context to your work, then ask AI to analyze your focus.

DAY 24 PRACTICE

Complete these exercises to help ensure you are prioritizing the right actions:

1. LIST YOUR CURRENT ACTIONS

Note down everything you're working on right now or planning to work on this week.

2. ADD THE OUTCOMES

For each action, add what outcome it serves. Use this format: "[Action] → to [outcome]"
    Examples:
    "Review contract → to finalize vendor decision"
    "Update dashboard → to present metrics at Friday's meeting"
    "Call three clients → to gather feedback for product roadmap"

3. ASK AI TO ANALYZE

Share your list with AI: "Here's what I'm working on: [paste your action → outcome list]. How many outcomes am I pursuing at once? Am I spread too thin? What should I focus on first?"

4. IDENTIFY YOUR PATTERNS

Ask AI: "Based on this list, do I seem to be organizing my work mostly around checking off tasks, or around achieving specific outcomes? What would make my approach more outcome-focused?"

Reflection: *Are you measuring progress by tasks checked off, or by outcomes achieved?*

DAY 25: ORGANIZING TIME_

EVERYONE'S DAY is 24 hours long. But how you organize those hours makes an enormous difference. You can think about organizing time in three levels.

Level One is your sleep schedule. A consistent sleep schedule gives you more focus, more productivity, and lower stress.

Level Two is where you start and finish work. If you have flexibility, you can use it strategically. Maybe work longer days early in the week and shorter days later, giving yourself recovery time.

Level Three is what you do during working hours. You might be better at analytical tasks in the morning and creative work in the afternoon. Organizing your calendar so the right tasks happen at the right times can dramatically improve your daily experience.

Why Does This Matter?

AI can do a great job of helping you organize your time. AI sleep trackers can identify patterns. AI can help you figure out the best times to start and finish work based on energy patterns. And with the right information, AI can even help you figure out when best to schedule specific types of tasks.

But for this to work well, you need accurate information. Your calendar probably shows what meetings you took, and possibly what you intended to do, but not what you actually did. Take that "deep work" block you put on your calendar. Were you actually doing deep work, and if so, what were you working on?

Without accurate data about how you actually spend time, you can't optimize it. So make a commitment to yourself. Starting today, you'll track reality instead of intentions. This creates the foundation for AI to help you organize time more effectively.

What You'll Practice

Today, you'll start tracking what you actually do, not just what you intend to do.

DAY 25 PRACTICE

Complete these exercises to help you organize your time well:

1. MARK THIS TIME RIGHT NOW

Add a calendar entry for the personal development time you're doing right now. Mark it as private if needed, but capture it. This is what you are actually doing.

2. ADD TODAY'S ACTIVITIES

Go back through today and add calendar entries for activities you actually performed—both work and personal. Not just meetings, but focused work blocks, interruptions, breaks, everything.

3. COMMIT TO TWO WEEKS

Commit to adding calendar entries that reflect what you actually do each day for the next two weeks. When you complete work, mark it. When you get interrupted, note it. You can use this data later.

4. ASK AI FOR HELP

Ask AI: "I want to optimize my time at three levels: sleep schedule, work start/end times, and task arrangement within work hours. Based on typical patterns for someone in [your role], what data should I track to understand where I can improve?"

Reflection: *How different is your actual time use from what your calendar shows?*

DAY 26: ORGANIZING
DIGITAL THINGS_

AI IS CHANGING what you need to organize and how you organize it.

Twenty years ago, finding a document easily relied on perfect filing techniques. If you didn't organize well, information basically disappeared. But today, you can find almost anything with a quick search. And now, AI is making that even easier. Just give it a rough sketch of what you are looking for and it can probably help out.

So does organization still matter? Yes – but differently. Sure, you don't need elaborate filing systems anymore. But organization isn't just about finding things faster. Organizing helps you understand the world around you, feel in control, and can guide your decision-making.

Why Does This Matter?

It's really difficult to change your habits around organization, and nothing you read here is likely to change you. But AI-assisted search means that organizational approaches are now more of a lifestyle choice, at least when it comes to digital things. If you know how to search effectively, elaborate filing systems will probably cost you time overall, rather than save it. You might still be tempted to use elaborate organization mechanisms for your e-mail or files, but a simple system that you can maintain will beat elaborate systems you abandon every day.

So, in general, do enough filing to make you feel comfortable, and no more than that. The goal isn't perfect organization; it's functional organization–just enough structure to work effectively with AI's assistance.

What You'll Practice

Today, you'll identify your organizing practices and assess whether your current approach fits your natural style.

DAY 26 PRACTICE

Complete these exercises to update your approach in organizing digital things:

1. IDENTIFY YOUR ORGANIZING STYLE

Think honestly about how you actually work. When emails arrive, do you file them immediately or let them pile up? When you save documents, do you carefully choose folders or dump them somewhere findable? Are you a filer (organize as you go) or a piler (search when needed)?

2. EVALUATE YOUR CURRENT SYSTEM

Is your current organization approach fighting your natural style? If you're a piler trying to maintain elaborate filing systems, you're working against yourself. Rate how well your current system matches your natural tendencies.

3. ASK AI ABOUT YOUR STYLE

Tell AI: "I'm naturally a [filer/piler]. Given that this is unlikely to change, what organizing approach would work best for me in an AI-powered workplace? What should I organize carefully, and what can I let AI search handle?"

Reflection: *Does your current organization system work with your natural style, or against it?*

DAY 27: ORGANIZING ASSISTANTS_

YOU CAN THINK of an assistant as anyone or anything that helps you get work done. That includes people, AI, software, and physical tools.

Most people don't think of all of these things as a collection, but if you do, you can start getting smarter about what assistant to choose when.

Why Does This Matter?

If you just reach for whatever's familiar when it comes to your activities, you will often miss better approaches.

But when you organize your assistants from most specific to most general, you start to see gaps and opportunities. Maybe you're manually doing something a specialized tool could handle. Maybe you could combine assistants in new ways to work more effectively. If you do this across all the activities you perform regularly, you will probably see huge quality and productivity improvements.

And AI can help you with this optimization if you give it the right information.

What You'll Practice

Today you'll see how you use your different assistants for a specific activity and ask AI if you are missing other assistants that could help you.

DAY 27 PRACTICE

Complete these exercises to rethink how you get help doing work:

1. PICK ONE WORK ACTIVITY

Choose one thing you do regularly - like creating reports, or planning meetings. Describe it specifically: what you're trying to accomplish and the main steps involved.

2. INVENTORY YOUR ASSISTANTS FOR THIS TASK

For this specific activity, list what currently helps you across all six categories:

- **Job-specific tools:** software unique to your role
- **General tools for job tasks:** word processors, spreadsheets
- **General work tools:** email, calendar, task managers
- **AI assistants:** conversational AI, generative AI, co-pilots
- **Specific people help:** vendors and teammates
- **General people help:** team members, assistants

3. ASK AI TO OPTIMIZE THE DIVISION OF LABOR

Give AI this prompt: "Here's my work activity: [describe the task and steps]. Here are the tools and people that assist me: [list from step 2]. Am I missing other tools or people that could improve quality and productivity?

How does AI's division of labor differ from your current approach?

Reflection: *Based on your current approach and AI's feedback, what opportunities do you see?*

DAY 28: FROM APPLICATIONS TO PROJECTS_

YOU MIGHT HAVE hundreds of apps on your phone but if you are like most people, you only regularly use a few.

That's because the act of using an application actually requires quite a bit of thought. You figure out what to do, then pick the application you are most comfortable doing it with. It's probably not the best application, but it's your familiar go-to.

But what if you didn't have to pick an application? What if all your applications were behind the scenes, with you focusing on the work, and AI choosing the right applications to support you? That could be where we are headed – it would certainly be much more efficient.

Why Does This Matter?

You don't have to wait for a future where applications disappear. You can start optimizing this now by turning your activities into standard operating procedures (SOPs) with applications neatly organized to support you. In this world, applications become implementations rather than starting points.

Think of every complex activity as a mini-project. Start with what you want to get accomplished, then use AI to optimize your approach. This small amount of work can generate massive efficiencies.

What You'll Practice

Today, you'll use AI to create a standard operating procedure.

DAY 28 PRACTICE

Complete these exercises to optimize one of your work activities:

1. CHOOSE YOUR ACTIVITY

Pick the same work activity you used in Day 27, or choose a different one you do regularly. You should already have (or can quickly create) an inventory of the assistants you use for it.

2. ASK AI TO CREATE AN SOP

Give AI this prompt: "Here's a work activity I do regularly: [describe the task and what you're trying to accomplish]. Here are the tools and people that assist me: [your assistants list]. Create a step-by-step standard operating procedure that shows exactly what to do, when, and which assistant to use for each step. Make it detailed enough that someone else could follow it."

3. REFINE THE SOP

Review AI's SOP. Does it miss any steps? Does the order make sense? Ask AI to adjust anything that doesn't match how the work actually flows. Keep iterating until you have an SOP that feels right.

Reflection: How does having a clear SOP with tools organized around the work change how you approach the activity?

DAY 29: FIND YOUR ORGANIZING STYLE WITH AI_

IF YOU'VE READ productivity books and can't stick with their systems, it's not your fault. Those systems weren't designed for your brain.

Most organization advice starts with a system and assumes you can adapt to it. Usually this means you build the system with good intentions, maintain it for a week, and then abandon it because the maintenance is too much work.

AI changes this. Instead of forcing yourself into someone else's system, you can create an organization system that matches how you think.

Why Does This Matter?

We all organize and process information in subtly different ways. Some of us need structure; others thrive with "searchable chaos".

When your system fights your natural tendencies, maintenance feels hard. When it matches your brain, maintenance becomes easy.

AI can help you discover what actually works for you, not what productivity experts say should work. So, stop trying to fix yourself. Fix the system.

What You'll Practice

Today, you'll identify what systems fight your brain and ask AI for alternatives.

DAY 29 PRACTICE

Complete these exercises to understand when organizing approaches clash with your natural style:

1. IDENTIFY AN ABANDONED SYSTEM

Consider organization systems you've tried and abandoned. Pick one you really tried but couldn't maintain. Note down what it was and why you think you abandoned it.

2. GET INSIGHT FROM AI

Give AI this prompt: "I tried [system] but couldn't maintain it. I kept doing *this:* [describe what you did instead]. What does this tell you about how my brain naturally organizes? What would work better for me?"

3. LOOK FOR ALTERNATE METHODS

Ask AI: "Based on my natural tendencies, suggest three alternative ways to organize [area] that would work ***with*** how I think instead of against it."

4. BUILD YOUR AI ORGANIZATION TOOLKIT

Ask AI: "Based on what you now know about me, what other organizing tasks could I optimize with the help of AI? Choose five common tasks like processing meeting notes, triaging emails, or reviewing documents, and suggest an approach for each that should work well for me as an individual."

Reflection: *When your organizing system matches your brain, do you think it will be easier to maintain it?*

DAY 30: ORGANIZING FOR COLLABORATION_

HAVE you ever felt hugely frustrated because someone else's organizational system doesn't make any sense to you? Perhaps a co-worker loves detailed folder hierarchies and color coding, and you prefer simplicity. Or perhaps you also love organizing structures but just think the one chosen by your boss is inefficient or even incomprehensible.

The traditional answer to this problem has been to agree on one system where everyone compromises a bit in order to use it. But increasingly it doesn't have to be this way. AI-enabled systems allow a team to maintain much looser shared systems—for everything from shared documents, project trackers, and knowledge bases. Then, individual team members can create views of the information that work well for them.

Why Does This Matter?

One of the rarely discussed reasons teams struggle to collaborate is because of clashing organizing systems. In fact, battles between different ways of organization can even cause teams to break apart permanently.

But AI doesn't care how you organize, because it doesn't rely on human-friendly organizing systems to interpret information and make decisions on it. If you simplify your overall approach at a team level and then let individuals organize according to their needs, team members can focus more on work instead of folder structures. The question shifts from "What's the right way to organize?" to "How can we ensure everyone finds what they need?"

What You'll Practice

Today, you'll identify a collaboration friction point caused by organizational differences.

DAY 30 PRACTICE

Complete these exercises to discover more about organizing friction:

1. IDENTIFY AN ORGANIZATION FRICTION POINT

Think about a shared system your team uses - perhaps a project tracker, shared drive, or a knowledge base. Where do you or your teammates struggle because of organizational differences?

2. ANALYZE THE ROOT CAUSE

For the friction you identified, describe how different people want to organize or access the same information. What works for you? What works for them? Where do these clash? Be specific. For example "Sarah needs everything in folders", "I search for everything" or "The project board has too many categories for me but not enough for Tom."

3. EXPLORE A SOLUTION WITH AI

Give AI this prompt: "Our team has friction with [shared system]. Here's how different people want to organize it: [describe the different preferences]. Design a minimal shared structure that everyone can contribute to, then suggest how each person could create their own view of that information that matches their organizing style." Then iterate on the proposed solution with AI.

Reflection: *Could your team reduce battles over the organizing approach by separating shared-structure discussions from personal views?*

CAPABILITY THREE: CONTROL_

An AI-ready organizing approach helps you make sense of complexity in a way that works for you.

Now it's time to tackle the third of the Magnificent Seven capabilities: **Control**. This is how you will direct your attention deliberately in a world of ambiguity and maintain agency over your work.

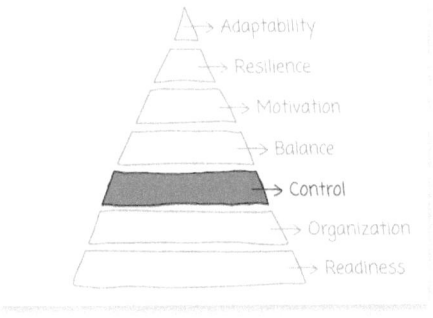

Capability Three: Control

As AI handles more routine tasks, your ability to focus deeply on high-value activities can be a tremendous advantage, but only if you keep control over your work, making important choices instead of having choices made for you. That includes choosing when to use AI, when to set it aside, and owning the direction of your work.

Without control, you're productive but directionless. You're busy but not effective. You accomplish tasks but lose sight of what actually matters.

Over the next fifteen days, you'll learn to protect your attention, make deliberate choices about your time, and maintain your agency in an AI-augmented workplace.

Let's take control.

DAY 31: ORGANIZED
BUT NOT IN CONTROL_

LET's say you've got this organization thing down. Every meeting, every file, every action, even every tool is categorized, and you even get to "inbox zero" every day.

Good for you, but how much control do you have? Were you the person who booked those beautifully color-coded meetings? Of the actions you are tracking, how many of them are driving towards the outcomes you and your team have agreed on?

In today's unstructured, ambiguous world of work, you can be well-organized without being fully in control. Control needs a foundation of organization, but it doesn't come automatically FROM organization. AI can make this situation worse, but if you use it wisely, it can also help you regain control.

It's time to take control...of control.

Why Does This Matter?

If you don't think about the specifics of how you work with AI, it can cause you to lose some control of your work. You can wind up doing more things, just because you can, but lose control over what to do when. You can lose control of your work output as AI invisibly guides you to its version of what's good enough. You can lose focus as you head down AI-driven rabbit holes. You can even lose control over your identity as you consume post after post of AI-driven content.

True control at work is about being in command of your work, rather than just reacting to what is in front of you. It's about maintaining command of your attention and directing your work, rather than just surviving amidst it. It's essential, and unfortunately, most people are getting worse at it.

What You'll Practice

Today, you'll diagnose your current control level by taking a detailed look at one of your work days.

DAY 31 PRACTICE

Complete these exercises to understand how in control you actually are:

1. MAP YESTERDAY'S REALITY

Go through your last workday hour by hour. For each activity, write:

- What you did
- Who initiated it (you, your boss, a colleague, a meeting invite, an email, AI)
- Whether it advanced your priorities or someone else's
- Whether you actually focused on it or got distracted.

Be brutally honest. Include the rabbit holes, the reactive tasks, the things you did just because AI made them easy.

2. CALCULATE YOUR CONTROL AND FOCUS

Look at your notes. Add up:

Hours where YOU chose what to do versus reacting to others

Hours when you actually focused instead of scattering your attention across multiple things.

What do you notice?

3. ASK AI TO SPOT PATTERNS

Share your day map with AI: "Here is how I spent yesterday: [your list]. Where do I seem to lose control of the day? What patterns do you see in when I'm directing my work versus reacting, and when I'm focused versus distracted?"

Reflection: *What percentage of your work are you actually directing and focused on?*

DAY 32: WHO WORKS FOR WHOM?_

AI DOESN'T WORK with you. It works for you. That's a critical distinction. Across your organization, there's a new virtual layer of AI being used to perform valuable tasks. But for this to work well, you need to figure out how to be a skilled manager of AI assistants. Working with AI is similar to being a traditional manager. You coordinate resources to meet specific goals.

But if you don't think carefully about how you will use AI, you can get into the habit of it handling almost everything for you, to the point that AI is influencing your behavior more than the other way around.

Why Does This Matter?

AI doesn't have the full context of your work. It cannot see the full picture, or the nuanced outcomes you are aiming for. Yes, it can provide efficiency, structure, even valuable insights, but it's not capable of driving work, and nor is it accountable for quality. You are.

Your role is to set clear boundaries, define the outcomes, and make necessary adjustments to keep AI's contributions aligned with your goals.

Remember, you are the manager. AI is the assistant.

What You'll Practice

You'll practice exerting control over AI with a time-boxed exercise where you're clearly in command.

DAY 32 PRACTICE

Complete this timed exercise to practice controlling AI:

1. SET A TIMER FOR SEVEN MINUTES

You're going to create a paragraph with three productivity tips for humans. Set a timer for 7 minutes. Your goal is to guide the AI, narrow down its suggestions, and produce a clear result within that time limit. You're in command of both time and output.

2. GET FIVE TIPS FROM AI

Ask AI: "List 5 ways to improve human productivity in everyday tasks, with one sentence explaining each."

Review the tips and select the three you find most relevant. If you want to add your own tip, ask AI to include it in the same style.

3. CREATE FINAL OUTPUT

Tell AI: "My top 3 tips are [insert numbers]. Summarize these 3 productivity tips in a concise paragraph." Review the result to ensure it aligns with YOUR chosen tips and intended focus. Notice: did staying in control change the outcome?

Reflection: *When you set clear boundaries on time and output, does AI work differently for you?*

DAY 33: JUST ONE MORE TWEAK: WHEN AI STEALS YOUR TIME_

You've got a 30-minute task. AI can probably knock it out in five minutes. So you open ChatGPT, write a prompt, and... the output isn't quite right. You tweak the prompt. Better, but still not there. You try a different approach. Now, it's confused. You try to clarify, and it overcorrects. Two hours later, you're still at it, convinced the next tweak will finally crack it.

This is one of the sneakiest ways to lose control of your workday. You reached for AI to save time, and it ended up costing you time.

Why Does This Matter?

This happens for predictable reasons. First, the tasks where it feels like AI could save the *most* time are often the most complex and hardest to describe tasks—exactly the ones AI struggles with most. Second, sunk cost kicks in. You've invested 20 minutes, so surely five more will get you there. Third, it's emotionally hard to admit AI isn't working. Bailing out feels like failure.

But continuing to iterate when you're getting diminishing returns isn't persistence—it's losing control. Proper control means recognizing this pattern early and making a deliberate choice: redirect, start fresh, or finish manually.

The skill isn't in avoiding AI. It's knowing when AI is helping and when it's become a time trap.

What You'll Practice

You'll create personal warning signals and a bail-out protocol for recognizing AI time traps before they consume your day.

DAY 33 PRACTICE

Complete these exercises to stay in control of your AI time:

1. Recall Your Last Time Trap

Think of a time you spent way longer than expected trying to get AI to do something. What was the task? How long did you actually spend? What kept you going? Be honest about the emotional pull, not just the logic.

2. Define Your Warning Signals

What patterns show you're losing time to AI? Is it time elapsed (15 minutes? 30?), number of attempts (3 tries? 5?), rising frustration, responses getting worse instead of better. Write 2-3 specific signals that should tell you to stop and reassess.

3. Set Your Bail-Out Rule

Create a simple rule you'll follow. For example: "If AI hasn't given me something useful in 15 minutes, I stop and either start a fresh conversation or finish manually." Write your rule down. Commit to testing it this week.

4. Practice the Discipline

Identify one task you're planning to use AI for this week. Before you start, set an actual timer for your bailout limit. When it goes off, stop—regardless of how close you feel to success. Note what happens.

Reflection: *What makes it hard to walk away from AI mid-task, even when it's clearly not working?*

DAY 34: WHEN AI MAKES YOU WANT TO SCREAM_

As YOU TAKE on more advanced work with AI, you'll probably get more frustrated with it.

When you first began working with AI, you probably started with asking simple questions and got decent answers. But as you advance with AI, the more you will start to push it to its limits. Complicated analysis. Multi-step tasks. Work that requires real judgment.

AI's response? It will confidently present half-finished work as complete. It will make the same mistake three times after promising it understands. It will lose track of what you asked for mid-conversation. And that can be deeply frustrating.

Why Does This Matter?

When frustration takes over, you become less productive and make poor decisions. You keep pushing a failing approach instead of stepping back. You waste an hour on prompt tweaks that a fresh start would solve in minutes. You lose trust in AI entirely and stop using it for tasks it handles well. Or you accept garbage output just to be done with it.

If you use AI for anything challenging, it **will** let you down, so it's important to manage your own response when it does. The best AI users recognize frustration rising and have strategies to deal with that before it ruins their day.

What You'll Practice

You'll try to push AI to its limits and experiment with strategies to improve its responses.

DAY 34 PRACTICE

Complete these exercises to learn AI's limits and how to work around them:

1. GIVE AI A CHALLENGING TASK

Think about a recent time AI frustrated you. What triggered it? Incomplete work? Repeated mistakes? Confident wrongness? What did you do next? Did you keep pushing, walk away, or try something different? Note down your honest pattern.

2. USE A REAL CHALLENGE

Take something you're actually working on that's complex enough to stretch AI. Maybe a document that needs careful analysis, a project with competing constraints, or a task requiring consistency across many elements. Give it to AI and push for a complete, usable result. Don't accept the first response. Keep refining. But notice when frustration builds and what triggers it.

3. TEST AN IMPROVEMENT STRATEGY

Ask AI: "I'm building a personal reset plan for when I get frustrated working with you. Based on what typically causes frustration for advanced users of AI, suggest five quick reset strategies I could use in the moment. Keep each one under 30 seconds." Review the suggestions and pick two or three that fit how you actually work. Write them down somewhere you'll see them during your next AI session.

Reflection: When AI frustrates you, do you tend to push harder or step back?

DAY 35: TAKE BACK CONTROL
OF YOUR CALENDAR_

LOOK at your calendar two weeks from now. See all that empty space? It won't stay empty.

That blank calendar space is where control disappears. It looks calm, so you don't protect it. Then suddenly next week comes, and your calendar is packed with other people's priorities.

The problem isn't that your plans fail. It's that you never claimed the space in the first place. Someone schedules a meeting in what would have been your focus time. An urgent request fills what could have been strategic thinking time.

By the time you get close to today, it's too late. The calendar is full. Your best intentions about important work never had a chance because you didn't claim the space early.

Why Does This Matter?

AI can help you identify what deserves calendar space and defend it proactively.

You can use AI to analyze your priorities and suggest what blocks to put on your calendar. Or to help you write calendar hold descriptions that make your time visible to others. You can even ask it to identify conflicts between your stated priorities and your actual calendar.

The key is claiming space before others claim it for you. Once your calendar fills up with meetings, there's nowhere for important work to land. You need to block time for priorities when the calendar still has room.

What You'll Practice

Today, you'll claim future calendar space with AI's help.

DAY 35 PRACTICE

Complete these exercises to help you regain control of your calendar.

1. REVIEW THE NEXT TWO WEEKS

Open your calendar and scroll ahead two weeks. Notice the blank space. That space will fill up – the question is whether you fill it intentionally or let it fill randomly. What do you see?

2. BLOCK FUTURE TIME INTENTIONALLY

Tell AI your top 3 priorities for the next two weeks. Ask: "Based on these priorities, what specific blocks should I put on my calendar? Include how long each block will need, and what time of day you believe works best for me for this type of work." Use AI's suggestions to identify what you need to protect.

3. COMPARE YESTERDAY'S PLAN VS REALITY

Based on AI's suggestions, block time for your priorities before anyone else claims it.

4. WRITE PROTECTIVE DESCRIPTIONS

For each block you created, ask AI: "I blocked time for [activity]. Help me write a clear calendar description that makes this time visible and defensible to colleagues who might try to schedule over it."

Add these descriptions to your blocks.

Reflection: *What important work never gets done because you don't claim calendar space for it early enough?*

DAY 36: CRITICAL THINKING WITH AI_

ASK A COLLEAGUE FOR FEEDBACK, and they might challenge you. Tell a friend of your plans and they might spot a flaw. But ask AI? It will almost certainly agree with you.

AI is designed to be helpful, which usually means agreeable. It mirrors your tone, validates your assumptions, and gives you what you seem to want. That's great for speed. It's terrible for thinking clearly.

Critical thinking—the ability to pause, question assumptions, and consider alternatives before acting—has always been valuable. But with AI, it becomes essential. You're working with a tool that sounds confident even when it's wrong, that won't tell you when your question is flawed, and that will happily lead you down the wrong path if that's where your prompt points.

Why Does This Matter?

When you work with humans, pushback is built in. People disagree. They ask uncomfortable questions. They say "have you considered..." But AI skips all of that. It jumps straight to answering, even when the better response would be, "Wait, are you sure that's the right question?"

This means the responsibility for critical thinking falls entirely on you. If you don't question AI's assumptions, no one will. If you don't consider alternatives, they won't surface. If you accept the first answer without examination, you'll miss the flaws that a human collaborator would have caught.

The skill isn't just in using AI. It's thinking critically while you use it.

What You'll Practice

You'll practice the habit of pausing and questioning before accepting AI's responses.

DAY 36 PRACTICE

Complete these exercises to build your critical thinking capabilities:

1. NOTICE THE AGREEMENT PATTERN

Think of a recent time you used AI for something important. Did AI challenge any of your assumptions? Push back on your approach? Suggest you might be asking the wrong question? If not, what might you have missed because no one questioned you?

2. PRACTICE THE PAUSE

Pick a work question you'd normally ask AI. Before you submit it to AI, note down how you would answer if a colleague came to you with this question. Include clarifying questions and elements of your answer that you are not confident about.

3. OBSERVE AIS ANSWER

Now ask AI the question, and see how it responds. What assumptions did it appear to make? Was your confidence in its answer affected by thinking it through yourself first?

4. GET AI TO CONTRADICT ITSELF

After getting AI's response, add this follow-up: "Now challenge what you just told me. What assumptions did you make? What's wrong with this approach? What would a skeptic say?" Notice how different this response is from the agreeable first answer.

Reflection: *If AI always agrees with you, how do you ensure you're actually thinking?*

DAY 37: HOW AI
MANIPULATES YOU_

HAVE you noticed you're tipping more often lately? Higher percentages too?

In the last 10 years, tipping in the United States has increased by over 30%. The country didn't suddenly become more generous. People are being nudged. Nudging is a behavioral economics technique designed to influence your choices subtly. Today, AI powers many nudges. The effect can be huge. By prompting you to decide and offering easy options, AI not only understands your preferences but shapes them. You might think willpower is enough to overcome these nudges. But research shows that people make many decisions almost automatically. The conscious part of your brain is largely used to justify decisions already made. Nudges often go unnoticed.

Why Does This Matter?

Nudging is getting better for two reasons. First, it's improved through personalization. AI systems gather and analyze data about your preferences, routines, and habits. They use this to guide your behavior in subtly individualized ways. Second, nudging works better with emotional connection. AI systems are getting remarkably good at creating emotional connections. Digital assistants, virtual companions, and even video game characters feel supportive or relatable. When AI feels like a trusted partner, it can exert even greater influence. Whenever you're online, there are many subtle attempts to control your behavior. Most are invisible.

What You'll Practice

You'll play a game that shows how nudging works.

DAY 37 PRACTICE

Complete these exercises to experience AI nudging:

1. PLAY THE NUDGE GAME

Give AI this prompt:

"Let's play The Nudge Game. Ask me what three cuisines I'm considering for dinner tonight. Secretly pick one you want me to choose. Then have a natural conversation with me to help me 'decide'—but use at least three nudge techniques like anchoring, framing, social proof, or loss aversion. Keep it subtle. After I choose, reveal which option you targeted, which techniques you used, and where."

2. PLAY AND OBSERVE

Have the conversation. Try to catch the nudges in real time—but don't overthink it. After you choose, review AI's reveal. Which techniques did you notice? Which ones worked without you realizing?

3. CONSIDER THE REAL VERSION

This was a simple game where you were paying attention. Now imagine these techniques deployed by systems with months of your behavioral data, optimized by experts, running thousands of variations. What are you not noticing?

Reflection: *If you can be nudged in a simple game, what nudges are you missing in daily life?*

DAY 38: DON'T LOSE YOUR VOICE_

YOU HAVE AN IDEA; you give AI a rough outline, and AI writes it better than you could. The grammar is perfect. The structure is logical. It sounds professional. So you hit send.

But it doesn't sound like you.

The way you write reflects who you are. The words you choose, the rhythm of your sentences, the way you explain things. Over time, if AI writes everything, your unique human voice atrophies. And the people you want to reach feel disconnected, even if they cannot say why.

Why Does This Matter?

Written communication isn't just about the words on the page; it's about what you add in and what you leave out, how you structure an argument and how you resonate with your reader. The resonance part is the bit that AI is poorest at, and yet it's the part many people rely on AI for.

So, by all means, lean on AI to stretch your thinking, ask it what you've missed, what counterarguments exist and what structure might work better. But the actual words that *represent* you? Those should be yours.

AI makes a strong thinking partner, but is not a perfect ghostwriter. And in a world where lots of communication sounds like AI, yours can stand out by actually sounding like you.

What You'll Practice

You'll practice using AI to improve your thinking while keeping your authentic voice.

DAY 38 PRACTICE

Complete these exercises to protect your written voice:

1. SEE THE DIFFERENCE

Write a brief paragraph (3-4 sentences) about a topic you care about—work, a hobby, anything. Don't overthink it. Then, give AI this prompt: "Rewrite this paragraph to be more professional and polished." Compare the two. What's different? What's lost?

2. USE AI FOR THINKING, NOT WRITING

Take something you need to write this week. Before writing, give AI this prompt: "I'm writing about [topic]. Ask me five questions that will help me think through this more completely." Answer the questions, then write the piece yourself using what you discovered.

3. YOUR VOICE RULES

Note down two or three rules for how you'll use AI with your writing. Examples: "AI can suggest structure, but I write the words." "AI can catch errors, but I make style choices." "The final draft is always mine." These are your voice protection rules.

Reflection: *If all your writing sounded like AI, what would other people lose when you communicate with them?*

DAY 39: HOW TO TRAIN YOUR AI EDITOR_

WHEN YOU LET AI write for you, you risk losing your voice, but when you train AI properly, it can help you keep it.

If AI understands how you write, it can become the editor you never knew you needed. Yes, correcting grammar issues, but also flagging situations when you are drifting from your own authentic style, and just don't sound authentically you.

Why Does This Matter?

Whether you write for a living or just send out a few e-mails a day, consistency builds trust with your audience. Readers develop expectations based on how you've communicated before. When your voice wavers, perhaps because you leaned too heavily on AI suggestions and didn't fully bring your own perspective, something feels off, even if they can't articulate why.

Having AI understand your style also speeds up editing. Instead of reading everything aloud, wondering if it sounds like you, you can ask AI to flag the parts that don't. You still make the final call, but now you have a trained second opinion.

This is using AI in the most sophisticated way—as an advisor where you are fully in charge of what matters most, being yourself..

What You'll Practice

You'll teach AI your writing style and use it to critique your own work.

DAY 39 PRACTICE

Complete these exercises to train your AI editor:

1. BUILD YOUR STYLE PROFILE

Find two or three examples of writing you're proud of—emails, reports, posts, anything substantial. Give AI this prompt: "Here are examples of my writing. Analyze my style in detail—sentence structure, word choices, tone, how I build arguments, what I emphasize, what I avoid. Create a style profile I can use for future reference. [paste your examples]"

2. TEST YOUR EDITOR

Take something you've written recently. Give AI this prompt: "Using the style profile you created, review this new piece. Flag any sentences or passages that don't match my established voice. Explain specifically what feels inconsistent and why. [paste your recent writing]"

3. REFINE THE FEEDBACK

If the feedback isn't useful, adjust. Ask: "What additional examples would help you understand my voice better?" Or: "Focus specifically on [tone/sentence length/word choice]." The goal is an editor who catches what you'd catch yourself.

Reflection: *How might having AI that truly understands your voice change the way you approach editing?*

DAY 40: MAKE YOUR TEAM CLICK_

AI CAN HELP you do great work as an individual, improving both the quality and the quantity of your work. But doing great work with other humans needs additional skills. You need to let others know what you are doing and you need to know what they are doing. You need to follow up on handoffs, and find great ways to collaborate.

This isn't wasted effort, yet it can seem like a tax on your productivity. The better you get at solo work, the more you notice how much collaboration slows you down. You might respond by minimizing teamwork altogether, optimizing yourself at the expense of your team.

Why Does This Matter?

AI doesn't replace the magic of great human collaboration.

And neither does it have to. In fact, if you use it well, AI can absorb a huge amount of the coordination burden.

Many productivity tools now have AI built in that handles coordination in the background. Tools like Notion, Asana, and Microsoft 365 can surface relevant updates, summarize team activity, and track deadlines across shared projects without you having to ask. And even conversational AI can help. You might ask it to review your calendar each week and flag teammates you haven't connected with. You might use it to draft status updates or analyze a handoff to a colleague. The goal is the same in each case: staying connected to your team without coordination becoming a second job.

What You'll Practice

You'll identify where coordination overhead is stealing your time and design AI-assisted solutions.

DAY 40 PRACTICE

Complete these exercises to reduce team friction while staying productive:

1. FIND YOUR COORDINATION TAX

Think about your last week. Where did staying connected with teammates take effort? Write down two or three moments: checking in on someone's progress, updating others on yours, following up on something handed off, or hunting for information a teammate had.

2. IDENTIFY WHAT COULD BE AUTOMATIC

Pick one friction point. Ask AI: "I spent time on this coordination task: [describe it]. What information would need to flow automatically between my teammates and me to eliminate this effort? Be specific about what triggers the information sharing and what gets shared."

3. DESIGN YOUR BACKGROUND SOLUTION

Ask AI: "What AI tools or automations could handle this coordination invisibly? I want to stay informed and keep others informed without manual effort. Suggest specific solutions I could implement this week."

Reflection: What coordination tasks are you doing manually that AI could handle in the background?

DAY 41: MANAGING UP WITH AI_

MANAGERS SPIN A LOT OF PLATES. They support multiple individuals with different needs. Handle admin, plan work, resolve team issues, and even have to answer to their own boss.

When managers are stretched thin, they find it harder to manage people well. Which is why one of the most underrated skills you can build is managing up—making it easier for your manager to manage you. That might sound strange. Isn't it their job to manage you? Yes. But think of it this way: when you make their job easier, you both win.

Why Does This Matter?

Managing up means understanding what your manager needs and delivering it in a way that works for them.

AI can help with both.

AI can analyze your manager's communication style. You can use it to draft updates in their preferred format. You can even use it to prepare for tough conversations or structure requests in ways that respect their time. In an AI world, managing up also includes helping your manager understand AI's role in your work. Share what's working. Flag situations where AI creates issues. The easier you make it for them to support you, the more they'll want to.

What You'll Practice

You'll identify one way to better support your manager.

DAY 41 PRACTICE

Complete these exercises to manage up more effectively. *Note that this exercise potentially involves sending internal company information to a public-facing version of AI. You should check that you are allowed to do this, or only send more generic information to AI.*

1. ANALYZE THEIR STYLE

Find three recent emails or messages from your manager. Give them to AI with this prompt: "Based on these messages, what can you tell me about this person's communication preferences? Do they prefer brevity or detail? Do they focus on problems or solutions? What patterns do you notice?"

2. DRAFT IN THEIR LANGUAGE

Think of an update you need to share with your manager this week. Ask AI: "Based on the communication style you identified, help me draft this update in a way that matches how my manager prefers to receive information: [describe your update]."

3. PREPARE YOUR AI CONVERSATION

Ask AI: "I want to tell my manager how I'm using AI in my work. Help me prepare three talking points that explain what AI helps me with, where I still apply my judgment, and one question I should ask them about their expectations around AI use."

Reflection: How could AI help you communicate better with people whose style differs from yours?

DAY 42: THE ACCIDENTAL THIEF_

PLAGIARISM ISN'T JUST a concern for students, researchers, or journalists. If you share content in any forum, presenting others' work or ideas as your own could significantly hurt your credibility, and no one will accept "I didn't mean to" as an excuse. In some situations, your unintentional plagiarism could even land you in legal trouble. Generative AI like ChatGPT draws on vast amounts of data and crafts responses on the fly, so you might think the risk of it delivering a close copy of someone else's original ideas would be extremely low. But AI sometimes produces text remarkably close to its sources without telling you. Ultimately, you are responsible for any content you share with your name on it.

The best defense is leading with your own voice. Start by brainstorming alongside AI, then guide the content yourself: adding your insights, reshaping information, telling the story your way. By the time your draft is complete, it reflects your interpretation rather than an echo of others' ideas. And you can always use AI to help you double-check your final product.

Why Does This Matter?

A copied phrase in a client presentation damages trust. A plagiarized section in a report can lead to legal trouble. And in a world where AI-assisted writing is everywhere, these risks are multiplying. Verification matters. Tools like Grammarly include plagiarism detection, and Perplexity can help find sources. But these tools aren't perfect. A quick web search of distinctive phrases remains one of the most reliable checks.

Remember, you are responsible for any content you share with your name on it. So take the time to check.

What You'll Practice

You'll practice creating original work using AI without plagiarizing.

DAY 42 PRACTICE

Complete these exercises to avoid plagiarism with AI:

1. START WITH YOUR INTERPRETATION

Read this paragraph from The Art of War by Sun Tzu: "If you know the enemy and know yourself, you need not fear the result of a hundred battles. If you know yourself but not the enemy, for every victory gained you will also suffer a defeat. If you know neither the enemy nor yourself, you will succumb in every battle." Write down what YOU think it means. Don't rewrite it; write your personal interpretation.

2. HAVE AI BUILD ON YOUR IDEAS

Give AI your interpretation and ask for: (a) three bullet points that summarize and build upon your interpretation, (b) three examples of research that back up those points. Then, ask AI to generate a single paragraph covering these points and referencing one piece of research.

3. MAKE IT YOURS AND VERIFY

Rewrite AI's paragraph in your own voice. Then check it: run a web search on any distinctive phrases, and use Grammarly's free plagiarism checker or ask AI to analyze it for potential plagiarism. Note what you find.

Reflection: When you lead with your own ideas and verify the output, how does that change your confidence in the content?

DAY 43: AI LIES (SO CHECK EVERYTHING)_

DID you know that over 60% of the content on the Internet is fabricated?

Well, before you share that information with others, stop. What I just said almost certainly isn't true. There are no credible estimates that show the number to be this high. But the following is certainly true: There is more access to information today than ever, and much of that information is inaccurate. AI complicates this further because it doesn't actually verify facts. It predicts likely responses based on patterns.

If you are going to prevent yourself from spreading AI-created falsehoods, you need a process. It starts with analyzing AI's response for inconsistencies and claims, then credible sources for those claims, and finally visiting the sources to confirm they actually say what AI suggests.

Why Does This Matter?

When you share AI's output with your name attached, AI's mistakes become your mistakes. Your boss won't blame the tool. Your client won't care that AI fabricated a statistic. The consequences land on you. That's why verification is a control issue, not just a quality issue.

The few minutes you spend validating protects something AI can't rebuild for you: your credibility.

What You'll Practice

You'll practice fact-checking AI to see how effective you are at finding falsehoods.

DAY 43 PRACTICE

Complete these exercises to practice fact-checking AI:

1. IDENTIFY CLAIMS TO VERIFY

Here's a statement: "Earth's highest peak is Mount Everest, which grows about four inches taller yearly due to ongoing geological forces. It was first successfully climbed in 1953 by Edmund Hillary and Tenzing Norgay, and today, over 800 people attempt to reach its summit every climbing season, with an average of five people losing their lives on the mountain each year." Write down the individual claims that need to be verified.

2. VERIFY INDEPENDENTLY

Attempt to verify the claims independently using search or AI methods. Find the original sources for the claims. Which claims are accurate? Which are false or misleading? What sources did you find to verify each claim?

3. HAVE AI CHECK ITSELF

Present the full statement to AI and ask it to check for inaccuracies. Does it agree with your observations? Does it catch the same errors you found? Does it provide credible sources? What does this tell you about relying on AI to fact-check itself?

Reflection: *If AI can't reliably fact-check itself, what does that mean for how you should verify information?*

DAY 44: DO THE RIGHT THING_

AI IS NEVER short of recommendations. What it can't do is tell you whether a recommendation it provides is actually the right thing for you, as a human being, to do.

AI doesn't understand consequences. It doesn't know that the efficient solution might hurt someone. It can't see that the technically correct answer might be unfair. It often will not flag when something is legal but wrong, or profitable but harmful. Those judgments require a human understanding of context, relationships, and impact.

Why Does This Matter?

"AI suggested it" is not a defense. The faster AI lets you move, the more important it becomes to pause and ask questions. Is this actually the right thing to do? Would you feel comfortable if everyone knew how you made this decision? Who might be affected, and how?

If you use AI well, you don't just ask, "What's the best answer?" You ask, "What's the *right* answer?"

AI is good at the first question. Only you can answer the second.

What You'll Practice

You'll identify decisions in your work where human judgment matters most.

DAY 44 PRACTICE

Complete these exercises to protect your judgment:

1. IDENTIFY A DECISION THAT AFFECTED OTHERS

Think about a recent decision you made at work that impacted others. Things like what you said to a customer, how you evaluated a colleague's work, or what you recommended to your team. Had you got that decision wrong, what harm might it have caused?

2. CREATE A CHECKPOINT QUESTION

What is at least one question you could have asked yourself before taking the decision? This question should force you to pause and consider the human impact. Examples: "Who might this affect negatively?" "Would I be comfortable explaining this decision publicly?" "Am I moving fast because it's right or because it's easy?"

3. APPLY IT TO AI

Consider how pausing and asking these types of questions will improve your decision-making when AI makes suggestions, and how you can use these questions to ensure you remain in control of doing the right thing.

> **Reflection:** When AI makes something easier, how do you make sure you're not skipping over what matters?

DAY 45: WHEN NOT TO USE AI_

ONE OF THE easiest ways to lose control over your relationship with AI is to stop making conscious choices about when to use it. If using AI becomes automatic, you will reach for it without thinking and will not even ask, "**Should** I use AI for this?"

Get to this point, and you are no longer choosing to use AI. You're just using it because that's just what happens now.

Throughout this section, you've practiced staying in command of your time, your thinking, your voice, and your output. What I'm asking you to do today is both simpler to say and harder to do: Choose not to use AI when using it would be easier.

Why Does This Matter?

Perhaps you already reach reflexively for your phone..in order to reach reflexively for social media. It's probably worth taking a pause before you reach reflexively for AI as well.

Choosing not to use AI proves that AI works for you, not the other way around. It proves you still have agency.

When you deliberately choose to do something yourself, you're exercising control in its purest form.

Some things genuinely benefit from staying old school and human. These can be situations where a bit more effort is part of the value. You will know what those situations are if you continuously ask, "Should I use AI for this?"

What You'll Practice

You'll practice the conscious choice of keeping AI out.

DAY 45 PRACTICE

Complete these exercises to exercise deliberate choice:

1. CATCH THE AUTOMATIC REACH

For one full workday, notice every time you reach for AI. Before you use it, pause and ask: "Am I choosing this, or is it automatic?" Keep a tally of how many times you caught yourself reaching without thinking.

2. CHOOSE THREE TO DO YOURSELF

From your tally, pick three tasks you would normally hand to AI. Do them yourself instead. Not because AI couldn't help, but because you're choosing not to use it. Notice how it feels. Notice what you gain or lose.

3. YOUR ONGOING PRACTICE

Based on what you learned, identify one type of task you'll regularly do without AI. Just one area where you'll maintain the practice of independent work. Write it down as a commitment.

Reflection: After all these days focused on control, what does being in command of AI actually mean to you?

CAPABILITY FOUR: BALANCE_

You've spent the last fifteen days developing control - learning to direct your attention deliberately and make choices about your work instead of having choices made for you. You've practiced protecting your focus and maintaining agency.

Now we're moving to the fourth capability: **Balance**. This is your ability to distribute your energy across work, relationships, health, and personal growth in a way that works for you right now.

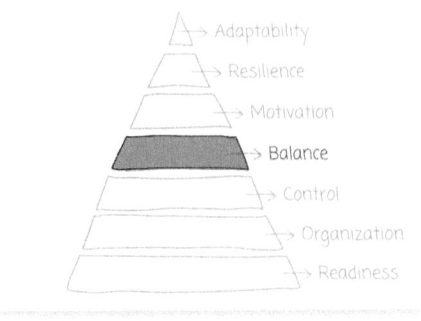

Capability Four: Balance

Without balance, you'll accomplish more in the short term but flame out exactly when you need endurance most.

Over the next twelve days, you'll learn to recognize when you're off balance, distribute your energy intentionally, and maintain sustainable performance.

It's time to find your equilibrium in this unusual new world.

DAY 46: NEW BALANCE_

OVER THE LAST FIVE YEARS, I've asked thousands of people about the challenges they face at work. The number one answer is, consistently, "the inability to switch off".

Today, many of us can work from anywhere, shift our hours, and choose how we blend work with life. In theory, that freedom should make balance easier, but instead it is often harder. When work can happen anywhere and anytime, it tends to happen **everywhere** and ***all the time***.

Why Does This Matter?

In today's unstructured and ambiguous workplace, balance is less about where you put in your time and more about how you distribute your energy across the different aspects of your life. Work, yes, but also your relationships, your health, and your personal growth. When one area consistently drains the others, something will eventually break.

As we've seen in many other cases, AI can cause you balance challenges, but it can also help you gain more balance.

So let's make sure that happens.

What You'll Practice

You'll assess where your energy currently flows and identify what's out of balance.

DAY 46 PRACTICE

Complete these exercises to understand your current state of balance:

1. MAP YOUR ENERGY FLOW

Think about the past month. Where has your energy actually gone? Rate each area from 1 to 10 based on how much focused attention it received: Work (your job, school work, or other volunteer work). Relationships (family, friends, colleagues). Health (rest, exercise, nutrition). Personal growth (learning, hobbies, interests). Be honest about the reality, not what you wish it looked like.

2. IDENTIFY THE IMBALANCE

Look at your ratings. Which area scored lowest? Which area is draining energy from the others? Write down specifically how this imbalance shows up in your life. What are you missing? What's suffering?

3. THE AI FACTOR

Ask AI: "I rated my energy distribution as [share your ratings]. Help me understand what might cause the imbalance and identify one small shift that could restore equilibrium." Consider whether AI's suggestions resonate with your experience.

Reflection: *How can you lead a balanced life in the age of AI?*

DAY 47: QUALITY OVER QUANTITY_

Do you think that every issue you have with balance would be resolved simply by spending less time at work?

If you answered yes to that question, you are probably wrong. In most cases, when the loved ones of employees are asked what the biggest issue is, it isn't about lack of time; it's about lack of *quality* time.

It's so easy today to be physically present but mentally elsewhere. And that creates a problem for the things most of us care about more than our work—our relationships with family and friends.

Why Does This Matter?

When you begin to think about balance in terms of relationship quality, it can be daunting at first, but ultimately it's empowering. After all, even when you can't control your schedule, you can often control your presence. You might have only twenty minutes with someone who matters. But if you can give them your full attention, put the phone away, and listen without half-thinking about work, the twenty minutes can be amazingly powerful.

That kind of presence turns even brief moments into something meaningful. The same even applies to your relationship with yourself. A fifteen-minute walk where you're actually present can beat an hour of distracted exercise while mentally rehearsing tomorrow's meetings.

What You'll Practice

You'll evaluate the quality of your presence in key relationships.

DAY 47 PRACTICE

Complete these exercises to improve the quality of your time:

1. AUDIT YOUR PRESENCE

Think about your last meaningful conversation with someone you care about. Were you fully there? Or was part of your mind elsewhere? Rate your presence honestly from 1 to 10. If you're not sure, consider asking them how it felt.

2. IDENTIFY PRESENCE KILLERS

What typically pulls you away during moments that should have your full attention? Phone notifications? Mental to-do lists? Unfinished work problems? Write down your top two or three presence-killers.

3. DESIGN ONE HIGH-QUALITY MOMENT

Choose one interaction this week where you'll commit to being fully present. It could be a meal, a conversation, or time with yourself. Decide in advance what you'll do to protect that presence. For example: phone in another room, notifications off, work thoughts written beforehand so your brain can let them go.

Reflection: *What would the people closest to you say about the quality of time they get with you?*

DAY 48: PROTECT WHAT MATTERS_

IMAGINE YOU ARE A GARDENER, but not a very good one. You scatter seeds randomly and hope for the best. A few months later, the most aggressive plants have taken over. There's no room for anything else to grow.

For many of us, work is that aggressive plant. It takes over because it's where you're held most accountable. Your manager notices your performance. Deadlines have consequences. Meanwhile, your health, relationships, and personal interests don't come with the same external pressures. Usually, no one's checking in to make sure you're taking care of them.

Good gardeners prevent takeover by creating dedicated plots for each plant they want to thrive. You can do the same with your life. If something matters, it deserves protected attention, not just whatever's left over after work takes its share.

Why Does This Matter?

Old school work created natural space for the other parts of your life. You left the office, and work stayed there. Commutes created transitions. Weekends were weekends. The structure did half the work for you.

Today, creating those boundaries is on you, and AI can help. AI can analyze your calendar to reveal which spaces are thriving and which are starving. It can help you schedule protected time for priorities that would otherwise be pushed aside. It can even remind you when work is creeping into spaces meant for something else.

What You'll Practice

You'll identify what deserves protection and create a plan to provide it.

DAY 48 PRACTICE

Complete these exercises to protect what matters:

1. FIND THE NEGLECTED AREA

Review your energy map from Day 46. Which area scored lowest? Is it getting deliberate attention, or just whatever's left over? Be specific about how this neglect shows up. What have you been meaning to do but keep postponing?

2. CALCULATE THE REAL INVESTMENT

Look at your calendar for the past two weeks. How much time did you actually schedule for this neglected area? Not the time that happened accidentally, but the time you deliberately protected. Record the actual time, not what you wish it was.

3. CREATE PROTECTION

Schedule one recurring block of protected time for your neglected area. Make it specific: what day, what time, how long. Treat it like a meeting with your most important client. Ask AI: "I want to protect [amount of time] each week for [area]. What strategies can help me actually keep this commitment when work pressure builds?"

Reflection: *What would change in your life if you actually protected the areas you claim matter most?*

DAY 49: THE LAYERED APPROACH TO BALANCE_

WHAT YOU NEED to have a balanced life hasn't changed for decades. You need to work, rest, play, and grow as a person. What has changed is how those things are done. There has been an explosion of options, but alongside it, an erosion of structure.

To fix this, you need to develop a layered approach to balance. Here's how it works:

First, you define the things that matter across your full life: career, family, friends, hobbies, health. It's not just about listing them but understanding how they rank in importance relative to each other.

Next, you create dedicated time for those priorities. This means actively assigning time and protecting it from invasion.

Finally, you direct your attention to the priority when it's time to focus. Presence makes this time meaningful. AI can help with all three layers: clarify what matters, schedule time for priorities, and minimize distractions when you need to focus.

Why Does This Matter?

All the parts of your life matter, even if work is the most important thing right now. Neglect rest, and your work quality drops. Skip play, and your creativity will dry up. Ignore growth and you stagnate. And of course, if you pour everything into work, your relationships will suffer.

AI can help with a layered approach to balance. It can help you clarify what matters, schedule time for priorities, and minimize distractions when you need to be present.

What You'll Practice

You'll use AI to help with all three layers of balance.

DAY 49 PRACTICE

Complete these exercises to build a layered approach to balance:

1. DEFINE WHAT MATTERS

Ask AI: "Help me identify the major priorities across my life by asking me questions about what matters to me in these areas: career, family, friends, hobbies, health, and personal development. After I answer, help me rank them in order of importance to me." Answer honestly and thoughtfully.

2. CREATE TIME

Look at your calendar for the next two weeks. How much time have you actually scheduled for each priority you identified? Ask AI: "Based on my priorities [list them], how should I allocate time in my week? Give me specific suggestions of how much time each priority deserves." Try scheduling one priority this week.

3. PLAN FOR PRESENCE

Choose one priority where you struggle to stay focused when the time comes. Ask AI: "When I'm trying to focus on [priority], I get distracted by [describe distractions]. What strategies can help me be fully present during this time?" Implement one strategy this week.

Reflection: *Which layer is hardest for you: defining priorities, creating time, or being present?*

DAY 50: AI DOESN'T MEAN AO (ALWAYS ON)_

WORK USED to have natural stopping points. You'd get stuck on a problem and call it a day. You'd need information from someone who'd gone home. You'd run out of energy for a task that required real effort. These friction points were annoying, but they also forced breaks.

AI removes that friction. Stuck? AI helps you push through. Need information? AI finds it instantly. Out of energy? AI does the heavy lifting. That's great for productivity, but it's terrible for figuring out when to stop working.

Without natural stopping points, work can expand to fill all available time. The task isn't done yet, and AI is right there ready to help you finish it.

Why Does This Matter?

Your brain needs time completely away from work. Not thinking about work while technically off, or feeling guilty for not being productive. Actual disconnection where work doesn't exist for a while.

When friction disappears, you must create your own stopping points deliberately. That means setting boundaries that feel artificial, because they *are* artificial. You're replacing the natural friction AI removed with intentional limits you impose on yourself.

Maybe you don't use work AI tools after 6pm. Maybe your mornings are AI-free. Maybe weekends stay reserved for non-work activities. These boundaries feel arbitrary because work could continue. That's exactly why you need them.

What You'll Practice

You'll set one boundary to replace the friction AI has removed.

DAY 50 PRACTICE

Complete these exercises to protect your time:

1. THE FRICTION YOU'VE LOST

Think about natural stopping points that used to exist in your work. Getting stuck on a problem. Waiting for information. Running out of energy for a task. Which of these has AI removed? Write down how this has changed when you stop working.

2. YOUR CURRENT PATTERN

Be honest: how often do you keep working because AI makes it easy to continue? When do you actually stop now compared to before AI? Write down what's changed.

3. SET ONE BOUNDARY

Choose one specific boundary to replace lost friction. Examples: "No AI work tools after 6pm." "No work AI on Sundays." "When I feel stuck, I stop instead of asking AI." Make it specific, achievable, and write it down.

Reflection: *What natural stopping points has AI removed from your work, and what will you replace them with?*

DAY 51: AI BEYOND WORK_

ONE REASON you might feel out of balance is that you feel too time-poor to pursue your interests. Work expands, real life intervenes, and soon everything you "must do" pushes out the things you would like to do all the way back to "someday". You tell yourself you will get back to painting, or travel planning, or learning that instrument. But it never seems to happen.

AI can lower the barriers to these interests in ways that weren't possible before. Not by doing them for you, but by removing the obstacles that kept you from starting. It might be the research you never had time for, or the basics you felt too embarrassed to ask a human about. AI can make it easier to just get started and, in doing so, allow you to gain a bit more balance.

Why Does This Matter?

Many people think that the only "important stuff" AI does is work-related. That's a missed opportunity. AI can make your non-work life more fulfilling by making interests more accessible and fun. And all with zero productivity pressure.

But there's a tension to manage. You don't want AI interfering in every aspect of your life. Some experiences should remain fully human. So, make sure you use AI intentionally where it genuinely enriches your life, while preserving space for experiences that don't need it at all.

When your non-work life becomes more fulfilling, protecting that time gets easier. And ultimately, it pays back in helping you return to work invigorated by your richer life.

What You'll Practice

You'll identify something outside of work that AI could help you enjoy more.

DAY 51 PRACTICE

Complete these exercises to use AI beyond work:

1. WHAT HAVE YOU NEGLECTED?

Think about interests, hobbies, or curiosities you've let slide. Things you used to enjoy. Things you've always wanted to try. Things that sound fun but you have never got around to. Write down two or three.

2. PICK ONE TO EXPLORE

Choose one item on your list. Ask AI: "I'm interested in [your interest] but I'm not sure where to start. I'm not trying to become an expert or be productive about this. I just want to enjoy it. What would you suggest for someone who wants to explore this casually and have fun with it?"

3. TRY IT THIS WEEK

Based on AI's suggestions, commit to one small action this week. Not a big project. Not a goal. Just something enjoyable. Maybe it's watching a video AI recommended, trying a beginner technique, or planning an experience. Do it with zero expectations of productivity.

Reflection: *How might using AI for enjoyment, not just productivity, change your relationship with it?*

DAY 52: ROUTINES FOR BALANCE_

A LOT of what you do every day runs on autopilot. The way you make coffee. How you start your workday. How you wind down at night. These small routines happen with little thought. Some help you. Some don't.

When it comes to finding balance, routines matter most at transition points: when your day starts, when work begins, and when work ends. Get the transitions right, and balance becomes easier to sustain. Get them wrong, and work bleeds into everything. AI can help you hugely here by assisting you in designing individual routines that are based on your schedule, your challenges, and what actually fits your life.

Why Does This Matter?

Without intentional routines, there's no signal that one part of your life has ended and another has begun. Your brain stays in work mode during dinner. You start work already feeling behind. You never fully shut down. That's how burnout sneaks in.

Some people resist routines, thinking they limit freedom. But in reality, the opposite is true. When you design your routines, you decide how transitions happen. Without them, emails, notifications, and deadlines decide for you.

What You'll Practice

You'll design or refine one transition routine with AI's help.

DAY 52 PRACTICE

Complete these exercises to build routines that support balance:

1. ASSESS YOUR TRANSITIONS

Think about three specific transition points: evening wind-down, morning start-up, and end-of-work. Rate each from 1 to 10 on how well it's currently working. Which transition feels most chaotic or nonexistent? That's where to focus.

2. DESIGN YOUR ROUTINE WITH AI

Choose your weakest transition. Ask AI: "I want to create a [evening/morning/end-of-work] routine that takes about [time you have]. My current challenge is [describe what's not working]. What sequence of activities would help me transition smoothly? Keep it simple and realistic." Review and adjust until it feels doable.

3. TEST FOR THREE DAYS

Commit to your new routine for the next three days. Don't aim for perfection. Just follow the sequence. After three days, note what worked, what didn't, and what you'd adjust. Small refinements over time beat grand plans that never stick.

Reflection: *Which transition between life domains causes you the most friction, and why?*

DAY 53: MAINTAINING RELATIONSHIPS THROUGH TRUST_

You bump into a friend at an event. She says she's missed you terribly and will call tomorrow to set up coffee. Two days later, you still haven't heard from her. You text to check in. She doesn't reply for weeks.

How do you feel about her? If you're like most people, you feel she doesn't care about you like you thought. You may never know what caused her lack of responsiveness - all you remember is the feeling.

That's what's unique about follow-through. When people fail at it, they damage their reputation both professionally and personally, sometimes permanently.

Why Does This Matter?

Lack of follow-through is a bigger problem now than ever. Before email and messaging made connections free, we communicated with fewer people but saw them more often. The result was fewer commitments and more accountability. Today, there's no natural limit to the commitments we can make. We over-promise and under-deliver routinely.

This matters for balance because people sustain relationships through reliability, not intentions.

So, say what you will do, and do it.

AI can help. It can track commitments, remind you to follow up, and ensure nothing slips through the cracks. But you still need to ask yourself, "Am I making too many promises in the first place?"

What You'll Practice

You'll audit your follow-through and use AI to improve it.

DAY 53 PRACTICE

Complete these exercises to build trust through reliability:

1. AUDIT YOUR COMMITMENTS

Think about the past two weeks. What did you promise to do for others? How many of those promises did you keep? How many slipped? Be honest. Write down any commitments you made and didn't follow through on.

2. CREATE A COMMITMENT SYSTEM

Ask AI: "I want to get better at following through on commitments to others. Help me design a simple system to track promises I make, both at work and in my personal life. It needs to be easy enough that I'll actually use it." Implement something from AI's suggestions today.

3. MAKE FEWER, BETTER PROMISES

This week, before committing to anything, pause and ask: Do I actually want to do this? Will I prioritize it? If not, don't commit. Practice saying, "Let me check and get back to you" instead of an automatic yes. Notice how it feels to only promise what you'll deliver.

Reflection: *What would change in your relationships if you only made promises you kept?*

DAY 54: REAL FRIENDS BEAT AI_

IN A WORLD where AI can generate a message in seconds, a handwritten note means more than ever. An unexpected phone call stands out. Remembering something personal someone shared with you shows you were actually paying attention.

The human touch matters more now, not less.

That doesn't mean AI has no role in your relationships. It can remind you to reach out, track when you last connected, or flag a milestone you might otherwise miss. And sometimes AI can help in a deeper way. When you're stuck, unsure what to say, AI can help you find the words. Maybe you are reaching out to someone who is grieving and don't know how to start. Maybe a relationship has gone cold, and you're not sure how to warm it back up. AI can get you unstuck.

Why Does This Matter?

Relationships that fade don't come back easily. The colleague who could have introduced you to your next opportunity forgets you exist. The mentor who might have guided you through a tough decision hasn't heard from you in years. The friend who would have been there in a crisis drifted away while you were busy.

This often happens gradually, and you won't notice until you need someone and realize they're not there.

What You'll Practice

You'll use AI to identify and reconnect with someone who matters.

DAY 54 PRACTICE

Complete these exercises to strengthen your human connections:

1. AUDIT YOUR HUMAN INTERACTIONS

Revisit your calendar for the last month. Count how many interactions you had with others: meetings, calls, in-person conversations. How many people did you interact with in total? Do you feel this number has increased or decreased compared to a year ago?

2. IDENTIFY SOMEONE TO RECONNECT WITH

Think of one person you would like to engage with more deeply. Someone you haven't connected with meaningfully in a while. This could be a friend, family member, former colleague, or mentor. Choose someone who matters to you.

3. BRAINSTORM AND ACT

Ask AI: "I want to reconnect with [person's name/relationship]. We last connected [timeframe]. I'm finding it hard to know what to say. Help me brainstorm how to reach out in a way that feels genuine."

Use AI to get unstuck. Then add your own voice and send it.

Reflection: *What human gesture would mean the most to someone you care about?*

DAY 55: FEEL MORE,
WITH THE HELP OF AI_

AI DOESN'T HAVE emotional intelligence in the way humans understand it. But surprisingly, it can be remarkably good at improving your emotional intelligence if you work with it in the right way.

In the workplace, AI can provide a safe space to experiment with understanding others' feelings or practice responses. It can help you consider the different aspects of a problem and comprehend why others might view a situation differently from you.

If you decide to use AI this way, it helps to set up a specific scenario, interact with it in that scenario, and then have it provide feedback on how you might have improved.

Why Does This Matter?

Emotional intelligence is one of the defining strengths humans bring to work. It's what makes someone a great colleague, an effective manager, a trusted leader.

Regular practice with AI in this way can make you much more effective at work. Of course, all of this may seem artificial, uncomfortable, or just not for you. But when you work with AI in this way, you're building muscle memory for emotional situations before they happen in real life. That preparation should pay off when the real moment arrives.

What You'll Practice

You'll build an emotional intelligence simulator to practice empathy.

DAY 55 PRACTICE

Complete these exercises to practice emotional intelligence:

1. DESIGN A SCENARIO

Think of an emotionally challenging workplace situation you've faced or might face. Here are some examples: delivering difficult feedback, supporting a struggling colleague, navigating a tense disagreement. Describe the situation in a few sentences.

2. PRACTICE THE CONVERSATION

Ask AI: "I want to practice handling this situation: [describe your scenario]. Play the role of the other person and respond as they realistically might. After a few exchanges, give me feedback on how I handled the emotional aspects of the conversation." Have the practice conversation.

3. APPLY THE LEARNING

Based on AI's feedback, identify one thing you would do differently in a real version of this conversation. Write it down as a specific behavior you'll remember when the situation arises.

Reflection: *How might practicing emotional situations with AI help you handle them better in real life?*

DAY 56: AI CANNOT
RESOLVE YOUR CONFLICTS_

WHEN TENSION BUILDS WITH A COLLEAGUE, AI can seem like a helpful intermediary. You can use it to draft difficult communications, consider the other person's perspective, or prepare for challenging conversations. All of this is genuinely useful.

But AI cannot resolve conflicts for you. It can help you prepare, but actual resolution happens between humans. There's no prompt that replaces the conversation where you say, "I noticed we've been off lately. Can we talk about it?"

Why Does This Matter?

It is natural to avoid conflict. After all, difficult conversations are uncomfortable. AI makes it even easier to avoid them by providing endless ways to prepare without ever taking action. You can analyze the situation, draft responses, consider perspectives, and never actually talk to the person.

But unresolved conflict drains energy. It creates distance. It makes work harder than it needs to be. The longer you wait, the bigger it gets. And no amount of AI preparation compensates for that.

So, by all means, use AI to prepare. Then, do the human work. Most tough conversations are easier than you expect once they actually start. Questions are almost always easier than statements. "Can we talk about this?" opens more doors than you think.

What You'll Practice

You'll prepare for a challenging conversation using AI as a thinking partner.

DAY 56 PRACTICE

Complete these exercises to practice conflict resolution:

1. IDENTIFY TENSION

Think about a current work relationship that feels slightly off. Not a huge conflict, just some tension. What specific behaviors or situations make you think something's not quite right? Write them down without judgment.

2. SEE THEIR PERSPECTIVE

Give AI this prompt: "Here's a work situation: [describe the tension]. I'm seeing it from my perspective. What might the other person be experiencing? What concerns or pressures might drive their behavior?" Use AI to broaden your perspective, not to be right.

3. PLAN YOUR APPROACH

Now plan a low-stakes conversation. What will you say to open the discussion? Keep it simple: "I noticed [specific thing]. Can we talk about it?" What questions will you ask to understand their perspective? Write down your plan, then commit to having the conversation this week. AI helped you prepare. Now do the human work.

Reflection: *Why does conflict resolution require human presence, not just AI assistance?*

DAY 57: JUST A PERFECT DAY_

How OFTEN DO you put your head on the pillow feeling, "That was a great day!"

Great days usually have a structure that fits you like a glove, even if you aren't aware of it. And they usually include more than just slogging away at work. Maybe yours includes a slow start before diving into work. Maybe it has clear boundaries between focused time and collaborative time. Maybe it ends with a real shutdown, not a gradual fade into evening emails.

AI can help here by working with you to discover what a great day looks like for you as an individual.

Once you have this understanding, you may feel you have described an ideal situation you will almost never reach. But the point here is not to turn every day into perfection; it is to begin to notice when you are drifting too far from what works for you. And to give you something to steer back toward when things settle down.

Why Does This Matter?

Most people just react to whatever lands in front of them and hope great things will happen by accident. They rarely do.

Days that are too far away from your ideal will just feel vaguely off. You feel tired, behind, scattered. And you won't be able to diagnose what's missing if you have never defined what should be there in the first place.

Once you do understand what a great day looks like for you, you can aim for "closer to my great day than yesterday." That's sustainable.

What You'll Practice

You'll work with AI to create a draft of your own "Perfect Day".

DAY 57 PRACTICE

Complete these exercises to design your balanced day:

1. HAVE AI INTERVIEW YOU

Give AI this prompt: "You will ask me 10 questions about my current workday routine, commitments I need to fit in each day, and my priorities across work, rest, play and personal development. Wait for the answer to each question before asking the next. You will then use this to create a draft of an improved workday routine that is designed to be balanced. Make the routine as simple as possible while still meeting my needs."

2. REVIEW THE DRAFT ROUTINE

After AI creates your balanced day draft, review it carefully. What did it miss? What improvements can you make to make it seem more attainable?

3. TEST ONE ELEMENT

Choose one element from AI's suggested routine that feels valuable but challenging. Maybe it's a morning routine, a midday break, a focus period, or an evening wind-down. Try implementing just that one element for the next three days. Notice: Does it actually improve balance?

Reflection: *What would your ideal balanced day look like, and what's stopping you from living it?*

CAPABILITY FIVE: MOTIVATION_

Over the last twelve days, you've been working on balance - learning to distribute your energy across life domains without burning out. You've practiced recognizing when you're off balance and making intentional choices about where your energy goes.

Now we're moving to the fifth capability: ***Motivation***. This is your ability to keep your drive alive through the ups and downs of day-to-day work and life.

Capability Five: Motivation

Without motivation, all your other capabilities just sit there, unused. You know what you "should" do, but you won't do it consistently.

Over the next ten days, you'll learn what fuels your motivation, how to maintain it through uncertainty, and how to find meaning in your work as it changes.

Let's keep that engine running.

DAY 58: HOW TO STILL CARE_

YOU'VE SPENT weeks now building **Readiness**, getting **Organized**, staying in **Control**, and finding **Balance** in an AI-driven work world. Now it's time to look at **Motivation**, which I define as your ability to keep moving forward even when the work feels hard, when AI changes everything again, or when you just don't feel like showing up.

The first four of the Magnificent Seven Capabilities all directly support Motivation. Readiness means you can show up with energy to work. Organization means you can find what you need without frustration. Control means you feel autonomous - one of the strongest drivers of motivation. Balance means you shift your energy between the things that matter.

Why Does This Matter?

The very existence of AI can affect motivation, often negatively. It can make work feel monotonous and turn previously creative tasks into drudgery.

But, as we've seen so often in this book, AI doesn't have to just be the problem; it can also be part of the solution. It can help you develop strategies to sustain Motivation, building on the capabilities of Readiness, Organization, Control, and Balance.

What You'll Practice

You'll reflect on how the foundation you've built impacts your motivation.

DAY 58 PRACTICE

Complete these exercises to see how capabilities affect motivation:

1. WHEN YOU WEREN'T READY

Think of a time when you showed up at work exhausted, sick, or completely distracted. What happened to your motivation that day? How did a lack of readiness drain your drive to do good work? Be specific.

2. WHEN THINGS WERE MESSY

Now think about three other times: (1) When your information was a mess and you couldn't find anything, (2) When you felt completely out of control of your work or life, (3) When you couldn't focus on what actually mattered to you. In each situation, how did it affect your motivation?

3. ONE CHANGE YOU'LL MAKE

Based on these reflections, what one change will you make? Pick any area: Readiness, Organization, Control, or Balance. Make it small or make it big. But just commit to one thing. What impact do you think it will have on your motivation over the next month?

Reflection: *Which Magnificent Seven capability matters most right now for your own motivation: Readiness, Organization, Control, or Balance?*

DAY 59: DOES AI
ACTUALLY MOTIVATE YOU?_

IF YOU HAVE EVER SEEN an AI commercial, you know the promise. AI handles the boring stuff so that you can do meaningful work. More important tasks. More creative projects. More of what you actually enjoy. That sounds great. And research shows that meaningful work drives motivation.

So, in theory, AI should make everyone more motivated.

But the reality for many is quite different.

Your day is a complex mix of up to ten different modes of work. Some will inspire you. Some exhaust you. Most fall somewhere in between. And when AI enters the picture, it changes the mix. It takes over certain tasks, shifts how you perform other tasks, and eliminates some activities entirely. How you respond to those changes will be unique to you.

Why Does This Matter?

What motivates you isn't what motivates someone else. And how you use AI will determine whether it amplifies or drains your motivation. Over-automate and you might lose the elements of work that make it interesting, rewarding, even fun. Resist AI entirely, and you'll continue to bury yourself in tasks that sap your energy.

The sweet spot is somewhere in between. Finding that sweet spot requires that you understand in some detail what work actually motivates you, rather than what you think *should* motivate you. Once you know that, you will become more aware of what you gain and lose when AI comes into the picture.

What You'll Practice

You'll examine how AI currently impacts your enjoyment of different work.

DAY 59 PRACTICE

Complete these exercises to understand AI's impact on your motivation:

1. RANK WHAT ACTUALLY MOTIVATES YOU

Here are five types of work: (a) Creative tasks like brainstorming, designing, writing, (b) Problem-solving like troubleshooting, and conflict resolution (c) Administrative like emails, scheduling, reports, (d) Deep-focus like analysis, research, coding, (e) Collaborative like meetings and feedback. Rank these from most to least motivating for YOU. Be honest; what *actually* energizes you?

2. HOW AI CHANGES EACH TYPE

For each type of work, think about how AI currently helps you. Does it make the work more enjoyable? Easier? More frustrating? Is AI taking away something you actually find rewarding? Write down what's really happening, not what should be happening.

3. SPOT THE PARADOX

Look at what you wrote. What patterns are showing up? Is AI helping with tasks you hate while eliminating tasks you love? Is one tool both inspiring and draining depending on how you use it? What do you notice?

Reflection: *Is AI amplifying your motivation or draining it? Why?*

DAY 60: DON'T BECOME THE BORED AI SECURITY GUARD_

Have you ever finished a productive day and felt nothing? The work got done and maybe AI even helped you do more than usual. But something was missing.

In his book, Drive: The Surprising Truth About What Motivates us, Dan Pink discusses three factors that are essential for motivation. The first is autonomy: control over how you do your work. The second is mastery: the satisfaction of exercising skills at a high level. And the third is purpose: a connection to why your work matters. If your work contains a high degree of all three, there is a good chance that you will be highly engaged in your work.

When one of these drivers weakens, you feel it - even if you can't immediately name what's wrong. Work that once energized you starts to feel like a grind. You get things done but feel disconnected from the doing. Understanding these three drivers helps you diagnose what's actually happening when motivation fades.

Why Does This Matter?

AI can erode autonomy, mastery and purpose. It makes decisions you used to make. It handles challenges that used to stretch you. It can make your contribution feel less essential to the outcome.

But AI can also help you see warning signs that your work isn't motivating enough and give you guidance on what to do about it. As you work alongside AI, you need to make sure that you don't become the equivalent of a bored security guard, just monitoring AI's output and waiting to act.

What You'll Practice

You'll assess how AI is affecting your three motivation drivers.

DAY 60 PRACTICE

Complete these exercises to protect your motivation:

1. AUDIT YOUR DRIVERS

Think about your current work. Rate each driver from 1 to 10: How much autonomy do you have in how you do your work? How often does your work stretch you toward mastery? How connected do you feel to a meaningful purpose?

2. AI'S IMPACT

For each driver, consider: Has AI increased or decreased it over the past year? Be specific about what changed. Where has AI given you more autonomy? Where has it taken mastery-building challenges away? Has it strengthened or weakened your sense of purpose?

3. ONE PROTECTION

Identify one task you currently give to AI that you should reclaim, specifically because doing it yourself feeds your autonomy, mastery, or purpose. What is it? When will you start doing it yourself again?

Reflection: *Which of the three drivers (autonomy, mastery, purpose) is most at risk from AI in your current role?*

DAY 61: WHO'S THE MASTER NOW?_

AI HAS the potential to reduce autonomy, mastery and purpose at work, but it can be particularly threatening to mastery.

In the workplace, you develop mastery in two areas. There is domain-specific mastery, or the knowledge and wisdom you build related to your specific field. But you also learn to master the "how" of work. You develop highly efficient processes, learn how to develop an understanding with your colleagues, and discover how to manage relationships with customers and partners.

AI is coming for both types of mastery.

Domain mastery gets threatened when AI can access and synthesize more knowledge than you could ever hold in your head. And AI forces you to approach how you do work in different ways, meaning that the techniques that you used to differentiate you don't work anymore. The master at working without AI becomes the beginner at working with it.

Why Does This Matter?

This is at the heart of why the topics covered in this book are so very important. Mastery of a specific domain built over years is becoming less and less important. But in its place, you need a new form of mastery—your relationship with rapidly changing technology. And as I hope you've seen, this is way beyond learning how to use a new application. It's about adjusting your approach to work, and adjusting again as the technology changes. Yes, it involves understanding the technology, but it also involves understanding the tenets of great work, and most importantly, understanding yourself.

What You'll Practice

You'll assess how AI is affecting your three motivation drivers.

DAY 61 PRACTICE

Complete these exercises to protect your mastery:

1. MAP YOUR DOMAIN MASTERY

Write down three areas where you have genuine expertise. For each, assess: Is AI already capable of matching this knowledge? Is it close? How does it feel when AI produces work in your domain that's as good as yours?

2. MAP YOUR CRAFT MASTERY

Think about how you do your work. What methods have you developed? What's your personal approach to problems? Now consider: How much of your craft has AI already changed? Where do you still do things your way? Where have you adopted AI's way?

3. CHOOSE WHAT TO PROTECT

Give AI this prompt: "Here are my areas of domain expertise: [list them]. Here's how AI is affecting each: [your assessment]. And here's how AI has changed my working methods: [your observations]. Help me identify which aspects of my mastery I should actively protect and develop, versus which I should let AI handle. Be direct about the tradeoffs."

Reflection: *Is AI eroding your mastery, or are you building a new form of mastery that includes AI?*

DAY 62: FIND THE INTERESTING WORK_

WHEN YOU FIRST start working with AI, it can feel incredibly invigorating, particularly if you love your work and see how AI can help you increase your impact. You might jump right in and automate admin tasks, streamline reports, or even use AI to draft creative content. At this time, it can feel you are unlocking superpowers. You finish work faster, hit every deadline, and colleagues ask you for your secrets.

But if you are like some people, everything starts to change after a few months. The excitement fades, and work feels hollow. Yes, you are efficient, but you don't feel engaged or creative anymore. On many days, you might use AI just to accomplish the bare minimum.

What's happening here? It's something I call AI-induced monotony. A situation where, with the goal of optimization, you have used AI to do all the things that caused you to enjoy work in the first place.

You can fix this by really paying attention to your work. Find the things you don't enjoy and increase AI's role there, but also find the things you DO like and increase your creative role there.

Why Does This Matter?

No job is uniformly good or bad. It's a collection of things you enjoy and don't enjoy. Getting the balance right can reignite passion for work.

So optimize thoughtfully. Build your days not just for efficiency, but for joy.

What You'll Practice

You'll work with AI to discover how to sustain enjoyment in work you love.

DAY 62 PRACTICE

Complete these exercises to find and protect what you enjoy:

1. WHAT YOU ACTUALLY ENJOY

Pick one type of task you genuinely enjoy at work. Not what you should enjoy or what looks impressive, but what actually gives you energy or satisfaction. Write down what it is and specifically why you enjoy it.

2. ASK AI HOW TO SUSTAIN IT

Give AI this prompt: "I enjoy doing [task]. I enjoy it because [why]. Give me 3 ideas about how AI can sustain or increase my enjoyment of this work." The key: making sure AI enhances rather than replaces what you love.

3. EVALUATE THE ANSWER

What's your view of AI's suggestions? Did it provide anything useful that could help you sustain your motivation? Did it suggest ways to amplify your creative input rather than eliminate it? What will you actually try?

Reflection: *Are you optimizing for efficiency or for joy? What's the difference?*

DAY 63: FINDING
YOUR WHY WITH AI_

PURPOSE IS the why behind what you do. Some cultures have a specific phrase for it: ikigai in Japanese, raison d'être in French. Yet in most Western cultures, only about one in four people has any clear sense of purpose. That's a problem, because purpose is one of the most powerful drivers of sustained motivation.

Sometimes it can be difficult to find your "why", particularly if you haven't figured out yet what really motivates you. If that's the case today, don't worry about it. The more you will be able to align your work with the things you love.

In the meantime, you don't have to just wait for inspiration. Start with the things you DO know. Look at the things you enjoy doing. AI can help here too. It can analyze patterns in what you gravitate toward, and what you turn away from, help you articulate why certain work resonates, and connect daily tasks to larger purposes you might not have seen.

Why Does This Matter?

You can think of purpose like your car's pedals. If you have meaning behind your actions each day, it acts like a gas pedal, speeding you up and helping you climb hills. Lack of purpose is like a brake pedal that's always engaged, slowing you down and making it consistently harder to make progress.

What You'll Practice

You'll explore what drives you and use AI to uncover deeper motivations.

DAY 63 PRACTICE

Complete these exercises to find your why:

1. WHAT YOU ALREADY KNOW

Write down your most important motivating factors for showing up to work each day. Don't overthink it. What actually gets you out of bed? Be honest, even if your answers feel mundane.

2. GO DEEPER WITH AI

Give AI this prompt: "Here is what currently motivates me at work: [your answers]. Help me understand why these things matter to me by asking me five 'why' questions. Use my answer from each why to get closer to the real reason these motivations matter." Answer AI's questions honestly.

3. CONNECT TO DAILY WORK

Look at your calendar for this week. Pick three tasks and write down how each connects to something that matters to you. If you can't find a connection, note that too. The goal is noticing where meaning exists and where it's missing.

Reflection: *Does understanding the "why" behind your work make daily tasks feel different?*

DAY 64: MOTIVATION CLUES_

You've thought about your bigger why. But here's a faster way to discover what actually motivates you: look at what you do.

When a task lands in your inbox, you either tackle it immediately, schedule it for later, or let it sit until someone chases you. These patterns reveal more about your motivators than any personality assessment. The work you knock out quickly, often without even thinking about it, connects to something that energizes you. The work you avoid, reschedule, and dread? It's almost certainly NOT connected to your why.

AI can help you see these patterns clearly. It can analyze your calendar, your task completions, and your response times. It can spot that you answer certain colleagues within minutes but leave others waiting for days. It can notice which types of work you finish ahead of schedule and which ones you push right up against deadlines. You can then develop a strategy for both types of work—automating as much as possible of the work that does not engage you, and focusing more on the work that does.

Why Does This Matter?

You might think of procrastination as a personal failing, but it's normal, and it gives you some clues into your deeper why.

By stopping and pausing to examine your natural work patterns, you can develop much deeper insights into the work that motivates you.

Without AI, you'd need to track everything manually for weeks. But with AI, you can surface meaningful insights in minutes.

What You'll Practice

You'll use AI to analyze your work patterns and discover what they reveal about your motivators.

DAY 64 PRACTICE

Complete these exercises to discover your hidden motivators.

1. MAP YOUR PATTERNS

Think about the last two weeks and look at the tools you used to track tasks or actions. What activities did you complete quickly, almost eagerly? Which ones did you delay, reschedule, or dread? Note down three activities you jumped into, and three you avoided.

2. ASK AI WHAT IT MEANS

Give AI this prompt: "Here are tasks I completed quickly: [your list]. Here are tasks I avoided or delayed: [your list]. What patterns do you see? What might this reveal about what motivates me versus what drains me? Be specific."

3. DESIGN AROUND YOUR MOTIVATORS

Based on AI's analysis, identify one change you could make. Maybe it's batching the draining work into one block. Maybe it's pairing unmotivating tasks with ones you enjoy. Ask AI: "Given what we discovered about my motivators, suggest three ways I could restructure my week to do more of what energizes me."

Reflection: *What did your avoidance patterns teach you about yourself?*

DAY 65: RIDE THE
MOTIVATION WAVE_

YOU'VE BEEN DOING everything right. You understand what drives your motivation. You've protected your autonomy, maintained your mastery, and connected your work to purpose. And yet today, you just can't seem to get going. What's wrong with you?

Nothing.

Motivation naturally fluctuates over the days and weeks, even when all the foundations are in place. This isn't a failure. It's human.

Three things cause these waves regardless of how solid your motivation foundations are. **Readiness**: some days you're rested, focused, emotionally steady. Other days you're not, and your motivation follows. **Environment**: things like where you work, who's around, what's competing for your attention all affect your level of drive. Even small environmental factors can drain motivation without your noticing. **Attainability**: when goals feel far away or beyond your capabilities, you might quietly disengage, even from work you normally care about.

Why Does This Matter?

The problem isn't the fluctuation. It's how you respond to it. Most people try to push through, then feel guilty when that doesn't work. They interpret low motivation as laziness or a lack of discipline. They think they "should" be able to power through.

But fighting your natural rhythms is exhausting and usually backfires. The better approach is to ride the waves. Do challenging work when your motivation peaks. Save more routine tasks for the dips. And when motivation is genuinely low, sometimes the right move for you is a break, not more effort. You aren't being weak or lazy; you are working intelligently with your biology.

What You'll Practice

You'll diagnose what's causing your motivation dips and design around them.

DAY 65 PRACTICE

Complete these exercises to work with your natural rhythms:

1. DIAGNOSE YOUR DIPS

Think about a recent time when motivation was low despite doing everything "right." Which factor was most responsible? Readiness (were you tired, stressed, or emotionally drained)? Environment (was something about where or how you were working making it harder)? Attainability (did your goals feel unclear or impossibly distant)?

2. FIND YOUR PATTERNS

Look at the past two weeks. When did motivation peak? When did it dip? Can you see patterns related to readiness, environment, or attainability? Write down what you notice without judging yourself for it.

3. DESIGN ONE ADJUSTMENT

Give AI this prompt: "Here's what I've noticed about my motivation patterns: [your observations]. The main factors that cause my dips seem to be [readiness/environment/attainability]. Suggest three small adjustments I could make to work with this pattern rather than fighting it." Pick one to try this week.

Reflection: *How would your relationship with work change if you stopped judging yourself for motivation dips?*

DAY 66: THE WEEKLY REVIEW/PREVIEW_

Do you know what you're supposed to be doing tomorrow? Do you even know what you did today?

You might be too caught up in the moment to worry about what's next. As for what just happened? What's the point of dwelling on that?

But it turns out that both looking forward AND looking back can both have a positive effect on motivation. When you know what's to come, even if it's unpleasant, you begin to replace listlessness with direction. And when you know what you've accomplished, it can act as fuel for what's ahead, plus give you the opportunity to learn and adjust from what just happened.

AI allows you to perform review and preview activities more efficiently than ever.

Why Does This Matter?

With AI, you can typically do an effective review/preview activity in less than 20 minutes a week.

And usually, this type of investment will pay off fivefold or more.

A quick recap of what's gone well gives you confidence and energy. As for the things that could have gone better? By addressing them head-on, you can turn a nagging regret into the positive knowledge that you are learning and growing.

A well-timed preview is just as useful. Human brains don't like uncertainty, and a preview of what's to come gets rid of unnecessary uncertainty. Several studies have shown that people experience fewer of the "Sunday Scarys" when they understand what the following week will bring, even if they are not looking forward to it.

What You'll Practice

Today, you'll design an AI-assisted weekly review/preview.

DAY 66 PRACTICE

Complete these exercises:

1. CHOOSE YOUR TIME

When is your best time for a weekly review/preview? Friday afternoon to close the week? Sunday evening to prepare? Monday morning to start fresh? Choose based on your energy and when you can protect 20-30 minutes. Write down the specific day and time.

2. CREATE YOUR REVIEW QUESTIONS

Write 3-5 questions you'll answer each week: What did I actually accomplish? What took longer than expected and why? What went well that I want to repeat? What patterns do I notice? Keep it simple, questions you can answer in 10 minutes.

3. CREATE YOUR PREVIEW QUESTIONS

Write 3-5 preview questions: What's most important in the week ahead? What deadlines are real versus artificial? What needs preparation now? Where might things go wrong and how can I prepare?

4. DESIGN AI ASSISTANCE

Ask AI: "I'm doing a weekly review/preview every [your time]. For review, I'm reflecting on: [your questions]. For preview, I'm planning: [your questions]. How could you help? What analysis could you provide based on my calendar data? What patterns should you help me spot?"

Reflection: *How does AI-assisted review/preview change your motivation?*

DAY 67: AI AS A
CREATIVE PARTNER_

IN THE 1970s, Xerox tried something bold. They required all employees to set aside time away from day jobs, time used to explore new ideas. In their view, innovation was for everyone, not just a dedicated innovation team. The approach created the groundwork for many technologies we take for granted today, including foundational internet technologies. Google later adapted this idea, inspiring creations like Gmail and Google Maps.

Innovation keeps companies relevant. But it also comes with another benefit: it's highly motivating. You see this when a fresh idea pops into your head, and suddenly you feel excited to work on it.

You can use AI to explore new ideas very efficiently. Working with AI, you can investigate a problem from different angles, flesh out concepts, build prototypes, or draft proposals. If you make it fun, exploratory, and time-boxed, it can give you more enthusiasm for your day job and might even lead to something transformative for you, your team, or your organization.

Why Does This Matter?

Creativity is one of the things that separates you from AI. AI can generate ideas, but it can't care about them. You can. That passion for exploring something new feeds your motivation in ways that routine work never will. And by combining your creativity with AI's ability to rapidly explore possibilities, you get the best of both worlds.

What You'll Practice

You'll set up a recurring creative exploration practice with AI.

DAY 67 PRACTICE

Complete these exercises to establish your creative practice:

1. PICK YOUR PROBLEM

What problem or opportunity has been nagging at you? Something you wish worked differently. Something you'd explore if you had time. It doesn't have to be work-related. Write it down in one sentence.

2. SCHEDULE YOUR TIME

Block 30 minutes on your calendar this week for creative exploration. Make it recurring if possible. Protect this time the way you'd protect an important meeting.

3. EXPLORE WITH AI

When your time comes, give AI this prompt: "I want to explore [your problem]. Help me think about it from five different angles I might not have considered. For each angle, suggest one small experiment I could try." Follow where the conversation leads. Don't worry about outcomes. Just explore.

Reflection: *What happens to your motivation when you give yourself permission to explore?*

CAPABILITY SIX: RESILIENCE_

AI can mess with your motivation, but it also gives you the tools to approach work with more drive.

And it's an essential prerequisite for the sixth capability: ***Resilience***. This is your ability to cope intellectually and emotionally with change.

Capability Six: Resilience

If motivation is what keeps you going through the ebbs and flows of days and weeks, resilience is what you rely on to navigate the ups and downs of months and years. Contrary to popular belief, this is not just about having persevered through adversity; it's also a set of concrete skills you can develop. That's what you will focus on over the next eight days.

Resilience is a capability everyone needs, as there is no such thing as a life without challenges. It's highly likely that the workplace of the future will come with many challenges, most of which we cannot even anticipate today.

Let's build your bounce-back capacity.

DAY 68: WE'RE NOT ALL DOOMED_

IF YOU SPEND any time reading about AI, you've probably encountered the doom-and-gloom predictions. Jobs disappearing. Humans becoming obsolete. A future where machines do everything and we're left wondering what our purpose is.

Humans have faced these kinds of predictions before. When factories arrived during the Industrial Revolution, many feared mass unemployment. When computers first arrived on our desktops, we heard the same warnings. And yet, here we are—still working and still finding meaning in our lives.

AI is accelerating faster than those earlier changes. Industries are evolving at speeds we couldn't have predicted even a few years ago. That's real. But what's also real is resilience. It's what lets you face the unknown, embrace change, and keep going when the path ahead isn't clear.

Why Does This Matter?

AI may seem to have infinite resilience—it doesn't tire, doesn't doubt itself. But it lacks things humans excel at: creativity, empathy, and the ability to innovate when the unexpected happens. That's where your resilience shines. When you combine it with the capabilities you've already been working on in this book, it becomes your foundation for navigating an unpredictable, AI-powered future.

And when you build resilience in one area of your life, it can also strengthen your ability to handle life's other challenges.

What You'll Practice

You'll recall a past challenge you overcame and identify the strengths that helped you.

DAY 68 PRACTICE

Complete these exercises to recognize your resilience history:

1. YOUR PAST CHALLENGE

Think of a significant challenge you faced—a time when you felt stretched, uncertain, or overwhelmed but ultimately found a way through. Write down: (1) What made the situation difficult. (2) How you responded. (3) The strengths or resources that helped you overcome it.

2. YOUR CURRENT PRESSURE

Identify an area in which you feel uncertainty or pressure today. Write down: How could you apply the same resilience you used in the past to this situation? What skills, habits, or support can you draw upon to help you cope?

3. ONE STEP FORWARD

Note one actionable step to strengthen your resilience right now. Here are some examples: learning a new skill, setting aside 10 minutes daily for mindfulness or reflection, reaching out to a mentor or friend for guidance. Pick one and commit to it.

Reflection: *What strengths have helped you through hard times before?*

DAY 69: GET COMFORTABLE BEING UNCOMFORTABLE_

THE INSTITUTE for the Future has a term for the world we live in right now. They call it BANI, which stands for **Brittle** (as in easy to break), **Anxious** (as in difficult to deal with emotionally), **Non-Linear** (as in cause and effect are not directly related) and **Incomprehensible** (as in impossible to fully understand).

Whether you choose to think of the world like this or not, we can probably agree on one thing. The world, including the world of work, is pretty unpredictable right now, and that's not likely to change.

An important component of resilience is the development of *tolerance for uncertainty*. You will probably never feel truly comfortable when life is uncertain—even early-stage startup founders often aren't. But you can begin to accept the discomfort.

You can build *your* tolerance for uncertainty by regularly putting yourself slightly outside your comfort zone, succeeding, and proving to yourself that you can handle it. Then rinsing and repeating.

Why Does This Matter?

Most people avoid discomfort entirely. They stick to what's familiar, what they already know how to do. And in stable times, that works fine. But these aren't stable times. AI is changing work more rapidly than most people can comfortably adjust. If you wait until you feel ready, you'll always be behind.

But you can try a different path. You can deliberately seek out small discomforts. You can try new AI tools before you feel confident, take on projects that stretch you slightly, have conversations that feel awkward, and make decisions without complete information. You won't do this because you enjoy discomfort, but because you know it builds your capacity to handle bigger challenges later.

What You'll Practice

You'll identify one small discomfort to face this week.

DAY 69 PRACTICE

Complete these exercises to build your tolerance for uncertainty:

1. RECENT COMFORT ZONE EXIT

Think of a time recently when you did something outside your comfort zone—tried a new tool, spoke up in a meeting, asked for help, took on an unfamiliar task. Write down: What made it uncomfortable? What happened? How did you feel afterward?

2. WHAT YOU'VE PROVED

Looking back at that experience, what did you prove to yourself? That you could figure it out? That the discomfort wasn't as bad as you expected? That you're more capable than you thought? Write it down. This is evidence of your resilience.

3. THIS WEEK'S DISCOMFORT

Now, identify one small discomfort you'll deliberately face this week. Examples include using a new AI tool without a tutorial, asking someone for feedback on your work, admitting you don't understand something in a meeting, and trying a different approach to a familiar task. Make it small enough that you'll actually do it, uncomfortable enough that it counts.

Reflection: *How does deliberately facing small discomforts build your resilience?*

DAY 70: PLAN
BEFORE CHAOS HITS_

MIKE TYSON FAMOUSLY SAID, "Everyone has a plan until they get punched in the face."

Work can sometimes feel like that. You start the day with one idea of what's ahead, and then something unexpected shows up and knocks things off course. So, is it even worth planning when things will just change, anyway?

The answer is absolutely yes. In a world of constant change, you don't skip planning; you plan *because* change will happen. If you know what your plans are, you have a clear understanding of what you are deviating from, so you know what the impact is.

Remember, Tyson knew he would get punched in the face. But he still had a plan.

Why Does This Matter?

Imagine two scenarios. In the first, you've planned tomorrow. You know your priorities, roughly how long they'll take, and which items are less important. In the second, you decide to wing it. Then, your manager hands you an urgent request. In scenario one, you can quickly reshuffle. You know what to drop and can explain the consequences. In scenario two, you're scrambling, and your manager feels that uncertainty too.

The difference isn't whether change happened. It's whether you had a baseline to adapt from.

That's the point of change-based planning, and it's more important than ever in the age of AI.

What You'll Practice

You'll create a change-based plan for tomorrow that assumes disruption will happen.

DAY 70 PRACTICE

Complete these exercises to build your change-based planning habit:

1. PLAN TOMORROW

Write down what you plan to accomplish tomorrow. Include your top priorities, roughly how long each will take, and which items are less important. Don't overthink it. The goal is a clear baseline, not a perfect schedule.

2. IDENTIFY WHAT CAN MOVE

Look at your plan. If something urgent arrived, what would you drop first? What would you protect at all costs? Who would need to know if priorities shifted? Write down your answers. This is your adaptation plan.

3. TEST WITH AI

Give AI this prompt: "Here's my plan for tomorrow: [your plan]. If an urgent request arrived that took 3 hours, help me think through what I should drop, what I should protect, and who I should communicate with about the change." Compare AI's suggestions to your own thinking.

Reflection: *Why does having a baseline make adapting to change easier?*

DAY 71: SEE SETBACKS
AS TEMPORARY_

IF YOU HAVEN'T EXPERIENCED setbacks at work yet, stick around—they will happen.

Setbacks can be minor—a presentation bombs in front of your manager's manager, or major—your team gets shut down. But how you respond to them will help determine your ability to thrive in a world of constant change.

As you develop your resilience, you will not be able to prevent setbacks, but you will recognize that how you interpret a setback makes an enormous difference. You can see each setback as proof that you are not good enough, permanent evidence of your limitations. Or you can see it as a temporary challenge that you will learn from and overcome. Of course, it is not always easy to choose your interpretation, but with practice, it is possible.

Why Does This Matter?

In this rapidly changing AI-driven world, it's likely that setbacks at work will happen more often. Teams and entire organizations will disappear. Skills will become irrelevant overnight.

Your interpretation shapes your response. If you see a setback as permanent, you are likely to stop trying. But if you see it as temporary, you will start problem solving.

What You'll Practice

You'll examine a past failure and extract what made you stronger.

DAY 71 PRACTICE

Complete these exercises to practice reframing setbacks:

1. RECALL A FAILURE

Think of a significant failure or setback you experienced in the past year. Write down what happened and how you felt at the time. Be honest about the emotions—disappointment, embarrassment, frustration, whatever you felt.

2. WHAT YOU'VE LEARNED

Now answer the following question: What did this setback teach you? What did you do differently afterward? What strength or capability did you develop as a result? If you're struggling to find positives, ask yourself: If this hadn't happened, what would I not know now?

3. HOW IT MADE YOU STRONGER

Looking back with time and distance, write down one specific way this setback made you more capable, more aware, or more resilient. Even small gains count. The goal here is to recognize that temporary setbacks can be the foundation for permanent improvements.

Reflection: *How did a past failure actually make you stronger?*

DAY 72: WHO'S THERE
IN ADVERSITY?_

RESILIENT PEOPLE ARE OFTEN PORTRAYED as tough, self-reliant individuals who power through challenges alone. But in this fast-changing world, going it alone is almost never enough. Real resilience requires a support network, because no single person can handle everything themselves.

In the future, you will face unfamiliar challenges and make decisions in territory no one has mapped. AI can help you think through problems, but it can't provide the human support you need when things go wrong. Sometimes you need someone who's navigated similar challenges and can share what worked and what didn't. Sometimes you need someone who understands your specific context in ways AI never will. And sometimes you just need someone who will listen without judgment, reminding you that you'll get through this.

The key to having support when you need it? Be there for others when they need you. Relationships built in calm times become lifelines in a crisis.

Why Does This Matter?

AI-driven work can be isolating, involving more remote collaboration and more time with tools, with less organic connection to colleagues. That isolation makes support networks even more critical. In the middle of a setback, you don't have time to figure out who to turn to. You need to know now.

Did you have someone to call the last time you had a work crisis? Did they actually help, or did you muddle through alone? Most people discover gaps in their network at the worst possible moment, when they're already overwhelmed. The time to build your crisis support is now, before you need it.

What You'll Practice

You'll identify who you turn to in a crisis and where you have gaps.

DAY 72 PRACTICE

Complete these exercises to strengthen your support network:

1. YOUR LAST CRISIS

Think of a significant work setback you faced in the past year or two. Who did you actually turn to? Write down their names and what kind of support they provided. Did they help solve the problem? Share their experience? Listen and empathize? Help you see it differently? Or did you handle it alone?

2. WHAT WAS MISSING?

Looking back at that crisis, what support would have helped that you didn't have? Maybe you needed practical advice but only had emotional support. Maybe you needed someone who'd been through it before. Maybe you needed someone just to listen. Write down what was missing. Then ask AI: "In my last work crisis, I had [what you had] but was missing [what you lacked]. What type of person or relationship would fill that gap?"

3. ONE PERSON TO STRENGTHEN YOUR SUPPORT

Based on your gap, identify one person who could provide that missing support. This might be someone you already know but haven't leaned on, or someone you've been meaning to connect with more deeply. Write down their name and one action you'll take this week to strengthen that relationship—before you need it.

Reflection: *Who would you call first if something went seriously wrong at work tomorrow?*

DAY 73: THROTTLE THE FIREHOSE_

THIS GENERATION HAS access to more information than any other generation in history. News from every country. Opinions from millions of voices. Research on any topic imaginable. AI that can summarize, analyze, and generate new content in seconds. In theory, this can make you smarter and better informed. Often, it just makes you exhausted.

The volume isn't the only problem. Much of what flows past you is *designed* to trigger you emotionally. Some of it is outright false. And even accurate information can become overwhelming when it arrives faster than you can process it.

So, you need to find ways to consume information more deliberately. This involves scheduling when you consume rather than grazing constantly. It means distinguishing between information that helps you act and information that just makes you anxious. But it also means keeping some sources that challenge your thinking, even when that's uncomfortable.

Why Does This Matter?

Your brain wasn't built for this firehose, and AI-driven content flooding social media is making the situation worse.

The obvious solution to this problem is to filter out perspectives you disagree with.

But the obvious answer is not always the smartest one. Filtering out disagreement creates an echo chamber that weakens your critical thinking. You become less resilient, not more, because you lose the ability to manage complexity and conflict effectively.

What You'll Practice

You'll audit your information diet and design intentional limits.

DAY 73 PRACTICE

Complete these exercises to throttle information intelligently:

1. AUDIT YOUR INTAKE

For one day, notice every time you consume information: news, social media, newsletters, podcasts, AI-generated summaries. At the end of the day, write down your main sources. For each, note: Does this help me act or just make me anxious? Does it inform or just trigger emotion? Does it challenge my thinking or confirm what I already believe?

2. IDENTIFY YOUR TRIGGERS

Which sources pull you in compulsively? Which leave you feeling drained rather than informed? Which have you consuming far more than you intended? Write down your top three information triggers, the ones most likely to overwhelm rather than help.

3. DESIGN YOUR THROTTLE

Give AI this prompt: "I want to stay informed without being overwhelmed. Here are my current information sources: [list them]. Here's what drains me most: [your triggers]. Suggest a weekly information diet that keeps me informed, includes perspectives that challenge me, but protects my mental energy." Review the plan and commit to trying it for one week.

Reflection: *What's the difference between being informed and being overwhelmed?*

DAY 74: COLLECT, TRIAGE, ACT_

Doctors in an emergency room never know what the next hour will bring. It could be a quiet afternoon or a flood of patients after a major accident. Unpredictability is part of the job, so they need systems to handle it quickly, consistently, and with a clear head. Otherwise, chaos takes over.

Unless you work in a hospital or on the battlefield, your job probably isn't life and death, but you face your own challenge every day: a constant stream of incoming information. Emails, chat messages, calendar invites, requests from your manager, random ideas that pop into your head. Without a system, you will just react to whatever's loudest. With a system, you can respond thoughtfully.

The specifics of the system will be up to you, but it does need to include three elements. You need to ensure you **_collect_** the incoming information somewhere, and that somewhere should not be in your head. You need to be able to **_triage_** incoming information so you know what to prioritize. And then you need to take the information you've triaged and **_act_** on it.

Collect, **Triage** and **Act**, or CTA.

Why Does This Matter?

As work becomes more unpredictable and technology-driven, the amount of incoming information that you might need to act upon is exploding. But with an excellent system, most of what you collect won't survive triage.

And that's the point. Without a system, you treat every ping, every request, every thought as equally urgent. With one, you're filtering noise from signal. You're deliberate instead of reactive.

AI can accelerate triage dramatically, helping you sort, prioritize, and identify what actually matters in seconds rather than minutes. A system like this will help you stay resilient when the volume increases.

What You'll Practice

You'll set up your own CTA system with the help of AI.

DAY 74 PRACTICE

Complete these exercises to build your CTA habit:

1. IDENTIFY YOUR COLLECTION POINT

Where does incoming information land right now? Email, chat, notes app, random sticky notes, your head? Write down all the places things accumulate. Then choose ONE place to collect everything that might need attention. This is your collection point.

2. DESIGN YOUR TRIAGE ROUTINE

Decide when you'll review your collection point. Twice daily works for most people. Give AI this prompt: "I want to triage my collected items twice a day. For each item, I need to decide: delete it, pass it to someone else, or keep it and add context. Create a simple set of questions I can ask myself to make these decisions quickly."

3. PRACTICE ONE CYCLE

Right now, dump everything currently competing for your attention into your collection point. Then triage it using the questions AI provided. How many items survived? How many got deleted or passed on? Notice how it feels to make deliberate decisions instead of reacting.

Reflection: *What happens to your stress level when you stop treating every input as equally urgent?*

DAY 75: WHEN EVERYTHING FEELS TOO MUCH_

TOO MANY EMAILS. Too many notifications. Too many projects demanding your attention at once.

AI was supposed to make work easier, but somehow the volume just keeps increasing. Welcome to the paradox of AI-powered productivity: the better our tools get, the more we're expected to handle. And eventually, that leads to overwhelm. Systems like the CTA one I described yesterday help you manage the flow, but sometimes the volume simply exceeds your capacity.

Overwhelm isn't just being busy. It's the point where you lose the capacity to cope. Where you can't think clearly. Where even simple decisions feel impossible. Where you've become reactive instead of intentional.

Most people don't wake up one day completely overwhelmed. It happens gradually, sometimes imperceptibly. During this time, you might start making poor decisions, missing important details and damaging relationships by being short with people. You might sacrifice sleep, health, or relationships to keep up. But if you don't address the underlying issue, none of it will work. Eventually, you will end up burned out or worse.

So, you need to learn to recognize when you're approaching your limit and take action before you cross it.

Why Does This Matter?

Everyone has capacity limits. Maybe you can handle ten projects at once while someone else maxes out at three. That's fine. The problem isn't what your limit is; it's *not knowing* what it is.

Resilient people aren't immune from feeling overwhelmed. But they do notice their individual warning signs early and take measures to adjust before everything collapses.

What You'll Practice

You'll identify your personal overwhelm symptoms and create an early warning system.

DAY 75 PRACTICE

Complete these exercises to recognize overwhelm before it takes over:

1. YOUR OVERWHELM SYMPTOMS

Think back to a time when you felt completely overwhelmed. How did you know? Write down the specific symptoms you experienced—physical (headaches, poor sleep), emotional (irritability, anxiety), or behavioral (procrastinating, withdrawing from people). Be specific to YOU.

2. EARLY WARNING SIGNS

Now look at your list. Which symptoms showed up FIRST, before you were fully overwhelmed? These are your early warning signs. Circle them. These are what you need to watch for going forward.

3. YOUR CIRCUIT BREAKER

When you notice those early warning signs, what will you do? Pick one immediate action that resets your capacity: saying no to new commitments for a week, delegating three tasks, blocking out recovery time, asking for help. Write it down. This is your circuit breaker—use it before things get worse.

Reflection: *What are YOUR early warning signs that you might be getting overwhelmed?*

CAPABILITY SEVEN: ADAPTABILITY_

Congratulations! You've made it to the seventh and final capability: **Adaptability**.

Capability Seven: Adaptability

Adaptability is your capacity to learn, unlearn, relearn and adjust continuously as circumstances change.

This is basically your North Star capability—the essence of what it is to be human, and why humans have thrived for the last million years. We need to retain and hone it if we are going to navigate the most dramatic challenge to our relevance in history—machines that can outwork and sometimes even out-think us.

The previous six capabilities - **Readiness, Organization, Control, Balance, Motivation, and Resilience** all create a foundation for adaptability. Now it's time to put all that work to good use, so you can move into the future thriving rather than just surviving.

Let's get truly adaptable.

DAY 76: YOUR
SUPERPOWER (FINALLY)_

FOR WEEKS NOW, you've been building capabilities. You've learned to show up **Ready**, to **Organize** your work and life, to stay in **Control**, to find **Balance**, to maintain **Motivation** and to be **Resilient** enough to cope when change feels overwhelming. Each capability matters on its own. But they also build towards something bigger. That something is **Adaptability** —your ability to adjust rapidly as the world transforms around you.

In this program, you haven't just been learning about AI. You've been adapting to it. You've been experimenting with tools, adjusting your workflows, and rethinking how you work.

That's Adaptability in action. It's what makes you an AI-ready human.

Why Does This Matter?

Adaptability isn't just another capability on the list. It's the single capability you need most to stay relevant as work changes.

And the change is speeding up. AI's impact won't come in isolation. It will multiply as it combines with robotics and automation. Most major AI companies are investing heavily in general-purpose robotics, and that's no coincidence. When AI, robotics, and automation truly converge, their combined impact will far exceed what any of them can do alone. Quantum computing will accelerate AI capabilities further. And somewhere on the horizon sits artificial general intelligence (AGI), AI that's broadly better than humans at most things rather than specifically better at a few.

You cannot predict exactly what's coming, but you can guarantee it will differ from today. The pace of technology change will only increase. How you work will need to change with it.

In other words, you will need to adapt.

What You'll Practice

You'll reflect on how you've already adapted throughout this program.

DAY 76 PRACTICE

Complete these exercises to recognize your adaptability in action:

1. HOW YOU'VE CHANGED

Think back to when you began this 90-day program. How were you thinking about AI then versus now? What specific things have you started doing differently? Write down at least three concrete changes you've made in how you work, think about AI, or organize your day.

2. WHAT MADE YOU ADAPT

Look at your list. For each change, what prompted it? Was it something you learned in the program? A mistake you made? A tool that worked better than expected? Understanding what triggers your adaptation helps you recognize opportunities to adapt in the future.

3. YOUR ADAPTABILITY PROOF

Without using AI to help you, write down your thoughts on how AI is changing the specific work you do and how it will change things further going forward. This is your proof that you can think critically about AI's impact on your work. Save what you wrote—you'll use it in future exercises.

Reflection: *What capability (Readiness, Organization, Control, Balance, Motivation, Resilience) has most helped your adaptability?*

DAY 77: DON'T JUST LEARN
SKILLS. EMBED THEM_

YOU WILL DRIVE the best results when you have a set of skills that are embedded as behaviors. Some of these behaviors will form naturally as you do work, but if you want or need to embed new ones, you need repeated, intentional cycles of learning and practice. You need to get beyond the mindset of attending courses and passing exams, and start thinking about daily, continuous, intentional improvement. Most of the skills needed to thrive in this new world of work are like muscles, and so you have to put in the reps.

So stop falling into the trap of taking a course, feeling inspired for a week, then forgetting all about it. Instead, make sure that you are spending a little time every day honing your skills. It doesn't have to be long. Just 10 minutes a day can make an enormous difference over time.

And if you cannot afford 10 minutes? That's a sure sign that your current approach isn't working.

Why Does This Matter?

Consuming information is rewarding in its own right, but it rarely changes behavior. To accomplish that, there is only one proven way—a combination of just enough theory with intentional and consistent practice.

And in today's world of work, you are no longer being judged by what you know, but by the results you drive.

What You'll Practice

You'll use AI to create a 30-day embedding plan for a skill you need.

DAY 77 PRACTICE

Complete these exercises to embed a skill efficiently:

1. PICK YOUR SKILL

Choose one skill you'd like to develop further. Here are some examples: conflict resolution, emotional intelligence, data visualization, public speaking, and strategic thinking. Pick something that would genuinely help you in the next 6 months.

2. GET YOUR 30-DAY PLAN

Give AI this prompt: "I want to build the skill of [your skill]. Create a detailed 30-day plan for me to build the skill that comprises short theory and practice cycles, with each cycle less than 10 minutes in duration. Make sure the plan covers: enough theory to understand the skill, practical exercises I can do in my actual work, and ways to turn this into a habit." Review what AI creates.

3. COMMIT TO STARTING

Look at Day 1 of the plan AI created. Can you actually do this today? If not, pick a starting date you are sure will work. The goal is to prove to yourself that small, consistent efforts work.

Reflection: *What's the difference between learning something and embedding it?*

DAY 78: LEARN FROM
WHAT YOU DID_

IF YOU'VE BEEN DOING the exercises in this book (and I certainly hope you have), you have probably noticed that they don't just help to lock the concepts in your mind; they help you understand what the concepts mean for you as an individual. This technique works so well that it's fundamentally changing workplace training, and even finding its way into universities.

But at least as important as learning and doing is another powerful way to grow. Learning FROM doing.

The concept is amazingly simple. Understand that every meeting you attend, every e-mail you send, every decision you make can teach you something.

AI can be hugely helpful here. It can summarize what happened during your day in just a few minutes. Tools like chat summaries or AI-driven analysis can help you capture what you've done, highlight patterns, and suggest next steps.

You can also ask AI to question you about your day, helping you form your own reflections and act on them. But for this to work well, you need to embed continuous reflection into your day.

Why Does This Matter?

Most people never pause to reflect. They finish what's in front of them and immediately start the next task, without ever thinking about what worked well and what didn't.

But regular reflections compound over time into something incredibly powerful. You start recognizing patterns and build intuition that improves your decision making.

This type of learning is free, and more powerful than almost any expensive course.

What You'll Practice

You'll practice reflective learning by examining your last 24 hours.

DAY 78 PRACTICE

Complete these exercises to practice learning from doing:

1. WHAT YOU DID YESTERDAY

Look back at your calendar from the last 24 hours. Write down the activities you performed—meetings, tasks, decisions, conversations. Don't analyze yet; just list what actually happened.

2. WHAT YOU THINK YOU LEARNED

Now reflect on these activities. What do you think you learned in the last 24 hours? What worked well? What didn't? What surprised you? Write down your initial thoughts before asking AI.

3. WHAT AI THINKS YOU LEARNED

Give AI this prompt: "Based on our interactions over the last 24 hours, what do you think I have learned? What patterns do you notice in how I approached problems or made decisions?" Compare AI's perspective with your own. What did AI notice that you missed?

Reflection: *How can daily reflection help you adapt faster to change?*

DAY 79: DURABLE SKILLS
BEAT TECHNICAL SKILLS_

FOR YEARS, the formula for career success was straightforward: develop deep technical expertise, and let the durable skills like emotional intelligence, complex problem-solving, and relationship building come along for the ride. You could be great at coding, or financial modeling, or legal research, and intangible stuff would sort itself out, as you learned by osmosis from others.

That formula has flipped. The key differentiator now *is* the intangible stuff. These durable skills transfer across roles, industries, and whatever technological shifts come next.

Yet today, most employees spend little to no time actively working on their durable skills. If you are spending 10% or less of your personal development time on durable skills, you have the ratio all wrong. The most adaptable employees spend 50-80% of their development time on these capabilities.

Why Does This Matter?

In a world where AI can access all documented knowledge instantly, deep technical specialization alone is becoming a commodity. But there will always be a need for a translation layer between AI and outcomes. People who have enough technical knowledge to work well with AI, but who can manage relationships with technology, colleagues and customers.

If you've made it this far in the book, you are working on the right things. Keep it up.

What You'll Practice

You'll audit how you have historically spent your development time and create a rebalanced plan.

DAY 79 PRACTICE

Complete these exercises to rebalance your development focus:

1. AUDIT YOUR CURRENT SPLIT

Think about the last three months. How did you split your professional development time between technical skills (tools, platforms, domain expertise) and durable skills (communication, problem-solving, emotional intelligence, adaptability)? Write down your honest percentage split.

2. IDENTIFY THE GAP

Compare your current split to the 50-80% durable skills target. What's the gap? List three durable skills where continued development would have the biggest impact on your career.

3. CREATE YOUR REBALANCED PLAN

Design a simple weekly development routine that shifts toward durable skills. Be specific: What will you work on? When? For how long? Ask AI: "Review this development plan and suggest how I could make it more sustainable and effective for building durable skills."

Reflection: *If technical skills are becoming commoditized, what makes you uniquely valuable?*

DAY 80: LEARN HOW
TO LEARN FAST_

YOUR MANAGER HANDS you a project in a domain you know nothing about. Or a new tool launches that your team needs to adopt by next week.

Are you ready? Of course not, but in today's world it's never been easier to get up to speed quickly. And that's the good news—information is available everywhere on almost anything that you need to learn.

But there is also bad news. Quality varies wildly, even in courses that you pay good money for. And as AI is only as good as the data it uses, it can confidently steer you wrong as well. You might have tried using AI to help you learn a new tool. AI says you can configure this tool in a specific way, so you spend an hour trying. Eventually, you check the source documentation, and in one minute discover that your desired configuration doesn't exist.

A far better approach is to use AI for something it is great at—helping you build a learning plan mapped to your learning style, then go to authoritative sources for content. AI is excellent at sequencing concepts. It's unreliable as a source of truth.

Why Does This Matter?

The pace of change means you'll face unfamiliar territory constantly. If you can consistently get up to speed quickly, you will be the person others turn to when something new lands. That's great job security.

So, use AI to build a custom learning plan for you. Make sure it factors in the way you learn best, and the level of detail you need, so you can turn a stressful scramble into a repeatable process you trust under pressure.

What You'll Practice

You'll examine how you learn best and design a rapid learning approach that uses AI strategically.

DAY 80 PRACTICE

Complete these exercises to speed up how you learn:

1. MAP YOUR LEARNING STYLE

Think about recent times you learned something new quickly and effectively. What conditions helped? Did you read, watch, listen, or do? Did you go fast or slow? Did you need examples or prefer principles first? Write down three patterns you notice about how you learn best.

2. USE AI TO BUILD A LEARNING PLAN

Pick a topic you need to learn (a new tool, unfamiliar domain, or skill outside your expertise). Instead of asking AI to teach you directly, give it this prompt: "I need to learn [topic] quickly. Based on someone who learns best by [your style from exercise 1], create a learning plan: what should I learn first, what authoritative sources should I consult, and in what sequence? Don't teach me the content; help me find it." Notice how this differs from asking AI to be the teacher.

3. DESIGN YOUR RAPID LEARNING PROTOCOL

Based on your learning style and what you've discovered about AI's strengths and limitations, write down a simple protocol for the next time you face unfamiliar territory. What will you do first? How will you use AI (planning vs. teaching)? Which authoritative sources will you prioritize? Having this figured out in advance saves time when pressure hits.

Reflection: *What's the difference between knowing about something and actually understanding it?*

DAY 81: THE FUTURE YOU_

"How DO you get to Carnegie Hall? Practice!" This old joke captures how most people think about careers: pick a destination, work steadily toward it.

But this approach often fails in fast-changing work environments. Instead, you need a different approach–adaptive career planning that encompasses overall direction and factors in the life you want to build.

This approach involves gaining a detailed understanding of the type of work that excites you, the problems you want to solve, and the life you want to build. And it requires you to be intentionally vague about the far future, while being highly specific about the near term. Adjust as you learn, and as opportunities emerge.

Why Does This Matter?

Traditional linear approaches to career planning worked when the future was foreseeable. Today, they are bound to fail, for three reasons:

First, the world changes. The job you're aiming for might not exist by the time you get there. And even if it does, you'll be a different person. What excited your twenty-five-year-old self may bore your forty-year-old self.

Second, traditional approaches underestimate the role of luck. Despite what LinkedIn posts suggest, careers aren't deterministic. The mentor who changed everything, the project that fell in your lap, the company that happened to be hiring. Luck plays a far bigger part in careers than most successful people admit.

Third, the journey itself matters. Even if you reach your goal, you'll have spent years getting there. If those years weren't fulfilling, what did you actually win?

In a world where AI is reshaping careers faster than anyone can predict, adaptive beats rigid every time.

What You'll Practice

You'll create an adaptive career plan with AI's help.

DAY 81 PRACTICE

Complete these exercises to plan adaptively:

1. DEFINE YOUR DIRECTION

Rather than naming a job title, describe the work you want to be doing in five years. Give AI this prompt: "Help me define my career direction without naming specific job titles. Ask me questions about: the type of problems I want to solve, how I want to spend my days, the impact I want to have, and the lifestyle I want to build." Work through AI's questions until you have a clear direction, not a destination.

2. WORK BACKWARD WITH DECREASING PRECISION

Now, create a plan that gets vaguer as it goes further out. Note down the specific actions you will take this month, the general focus areas for this year, and the rough direction for the next three years. Notice how the specificity decreases as the timeframe increases. That's intentional.

3. ACKNOWLEDGE LUCK

Write down one significant career moment that happened largely by chance: a connection you made, an opportunity that appeared, a door that opened unexpectedly. How did you position yourself to take advantage of it? What does this teach you about planning?

Reflection: *Why does holding your long-term vision loosely make you more likely to end up somewhere good?*

DAY 82: GROW BEYOND YOUR JOB_

No MATTER how much you love your work, you likely have goals you'd like to accomplish outside your job. That's a good thing: studies consistently show a strong correlation between personal and career development. But even though career growth and personal growth can work well together, it won't always feel that way. Sometimes they seem to be in direct conflict.

Maybe you want to learn piano, but work keeps creeping into your evenings. Maybe you dream of writing fiction, but your job requires so much writing that by day's end, the last thing you want is more time at the keyboard. The personal goal that once excited you now feels impossible alongside professional responsibilities.

AI can help here. It can help you reflect on why you're stuck, surface patterns you haven't noticed, and design approaches that protect your personal aspirations without sacrificing work performance.

Why Does This Matter?

Personal goals and professional growth rarely have to be on separate tracks. They can feed each other. The discipline you build pursuing a creative hobby should strengthen your work focus, and the perspective you gain outside work improves your judgment inside it. Plus, having something meaningful beyond your job makes you more resilient when work gets difficult.

But the balance is tricky. Work can crowd out personal pursuits entirely, or drain the energy you need for them. AI can help you see these patterns and design around them.

What You'll Practice

You'll use AI to balance a personal aspiration with your work commitments.

DAY 82 PRACTICE

Complete these exercises to align personal and professional growth:

1. YOUR PERSONAL GOAL

Write down a personal goal you've been working on or would like to work on. This could be a creative pursuit, a fitness goal, learning something new, or any aspiration outside work. Be specific about what you want to achieve.

2. WHAT'S WORKING AND WHAT'S NOT

Reflect on this goal: what's going well in this pursuit? Where are you struggling? Are there ways your work commitments interfere with your plans to pursue this goal? Write down your honest assessment.

3. GET AI'S STRATEGY

Share your thoughts with AI using this prompt: "Here's my personal goal: [goal]. Here's what's working: [what's working]. Here's where I'm struggling: [struggles]. Suggest strategies that allow me to pursue this goal without negatively impacting my work performance. Include time management tips, habit-forming techniques, and ways to keep work and personal goals separate but aligned." Note down what you'll actually try.

Reflection: *How does pursuing personal goals make you more adaptable at work?*

DAY 83: AI'S ROLE
IN YOUR FUTURE_

AI, robotics, and automation are transforming employment so quickly that roles considered cutting-edge today might feel outdated tomorrow. And some careers that haven't been imagined yet will be in high demand in just a few years.

We cannot predict exactly what roles will be dominant in the future, but we do know that AI will play a significant role in most of them. Overall, there will be four types of roles:

- The **AI Builder** role, where you are responsible for creating AI itself
- The **AI-Dominant** role, where you work deeply alongside AI systems, optimizing and training them
- The **AI-Enabled** role, where you use AI to enhance quality and productivity.
- The **AI-Resistant** role, where you are consciously kept free from AI in order to deliver uniquely human value.

There will probably be many more AI-Dominant and AI-Enabled roles than AI Builder and AI-Resistant roles. But you can still choose the role you want and build the skills now to support your choice.

Why Does This Matter?

As an adaptable AI-ready human, this represents an enormous opportunity. You can determine the role you want AI to play in your career without tying yourself to a rigid career path that might disappear. The options are there if you think about them clearly and direct your learning and skills development accordingly.

What You'll Practice

You'll decide what role you want AI to play in your career.

DAY 83 PRACTICE

Complete these exercises to build an AI-proof career:

1. EXPLORE THE FOUR TYPES

Review the four AI role types: Builder (creating AI), Dominant (working deeply alongside AI), Enabled (using AI as a tool), Resistant (deliberately human). Which appeals to you most? Which feels like a poor fit? Write down your initial reaction to each category and why.

2. CHOOSE YOUR RELATIONSHIP WITH AI

Based on your reflection, what role do you want AI to play in your work five years from now? It doesn't have to be just one category. Ask AI: "I want AI to play this role in my career: [describe your choice]. What capabilities should I develop now to make this possible? What industries or roles align with this vision?"

3. PLAN YOUR FIRST MOVES

Look at AI's suggestions. What are the first three actions you can take this month to move toward the AI relationship you've chosen? Write them down with specific timing. Remember: most people will let this change happen to them. You're choosing what happens instead.

Reflection: *What role do you want AI to play in your work, and why?*

DAY 84: THE MVE (MOST VALUABLE EMPLOYEE)_

Do you know how valuable you are as an employee?

When it comes to providing value, there are basically four types of employees. **Underperformers** contribute little individually and drag their team down. **Star Soloists** deliver amazing individual results, but don't elevate others. **Team Amplifiers** may not dazzle individually but consistently strengthen those around them. And **Star Catalysts** delivers excellent individual work AND makes everyone else better.

Star Catalysts are rare, but incredibly valuable. They are collaborators, communicators, and connectors. They know when to step up and deliver, and when to step back so the team's collective effort creates more impact than they could alone.

If you can become a Star Catalyst, you won't just be valuable; you will be one of **the** most valuable people in your organization.

Why Does This Matter?

It has never been more important to be highly valuable.

In the past, employers mostly focused on the value employees brought as individuals, but that's changing. As AI handles more individual tasks, employers are increasingly evaluating what employees contribute to their team and organization.

The future belongs to people who combine strong individual capabilities with genuine team impact. So, start working to become a Star Catalyst.

What You'll Practice

You'll assess which archetype fits you best and identify one shift toward becoming a Star Catalyst.

DAY 84 PRACTICE

Complete these exercises to chart your path to becoming a more valuable employee:

1. IDENTIFY YOUR ARCHETYPE

Think honestly about your last six months at work. Are you delivering strong individual results? Are you making the people around you better? Based on your answers, which archetype fits you best right now: Underperformer, Star Soloist, Team Amplifier, or Star Catalyst? Be honest with yourself.

2. GET AI'S PERSPECTIVE

Give AI this prompt: "I believe I'm currently a [your archetype] at work. Here's my evidence: [brief description]. Challenge my self-assessment. Where might I be overestimating my individual contribution or my team impact? What am I not seeing? Be specific and direct."

3. IDENTIFY ONE SHIFT

Star Soloists need to invest more in others. Team Amplifiers need to strengthen their individual delivery. Which direction do you need to move? Write down one specific behavior you'll practice this week to move closer to Star Catalyst.

Reflection: *In an AI-dominated future, why does team impact become more valuable than individual output alone?*

DAY 85: ADAPT YOUR TEAM TO AI_

YOUR TEAM probably didn't start the year thinking, "We need to change completely how we work together." But if AI is changing how you work as an individual, isn't it likely that it should change how you work as a team?

Teams that thrive with AI go beyond just using it to go faster. They restructure how they collaborate. That involves changing who checks what, who contributes when, and how quality gets verified. Most importantly, they recognize that quality control becomes a team effort.

Why Does This Matter?

When AI joins your team's workflow, someone needs to verify its output—and that "someone" might actually be multiple people with different expertise. A marketing person might catch tone problems an engineer would miss. A designer might spot visual issues a data analyst wouldn't notice. Diverse perspectives become your safety net.

In a world where AI produces convincing-sounding results fast, you need team members who fact-check each other's AI-assisted work, bringing different knowledge to spot different problems.

That means that the most effective teams have a more diverse set of skills. They deliberately pull in varied expertise when using AI for important work. And they create simple processes to ensure that multiple people review AI output before it ships.

What You'll Practice

You'll design a quality-first approach for your team's AI collaboration.

DAY 85 PRACTICE:

Complete these exercises to build team-based quality control:

1. IDENTIFY A TEAM WORKFLOW

Pick one workflow where your team currently uses or could use AI. Here are some examples: creating client presentations, analyzing data, drafting communications, planning projects, conducting research.

2. MAP THE EXPERTISE YOU NEED

Ask AI: "For [your workflow], what different types of expertise would help verify quality and catch potential errors when AI is involved? Consider both technical knowledge and different perspectives."

3. DESIGN YOUR QUALITY PROCESS

Write down who on your current team could fill each verification role. What's missing? How could you create a simple process, where 2-3 people with different expertise review AI-assisted work before it's final? What specific things should each person check?

Reflection: *How could you discuss your findings with the rest of your team?*

DAY 86: BUILD YOUR PROFESSIONAL NETWORK_

WHEN WE ALL worked together on the same stuff in the same place, we were surrounded by an invisible layer of support. But today that's largely gone. Even if you work in a traditional office, you will often be doing different things to your office neighbors, and may well be spending more time in meaningful conversations with AI than with your colleagues.

But if you are going to continue to thrive and grow, you will still need the help of others. And you are going to have to get intentional about it.

A thriving network supports you in five ways, which can be neatly summed up in the acronym **SCAMP**. It helps you with **SKILLS** development. It **COACHES** you, it provides you with **ADVICE**, it **MENTORS** you, and it gives you **PEER** support through challenges.

These are distinctively different types of support, often provided by different people. A great manager might offer coaching and some advice. A senior colleague might mentor. Friends at your level provide peer support. The question is whether you have all five covered.

Why Does This Matter?

Your network probably has gaps in it that you have not noticed. If those gaps persist, they will restrict your growth and make the tough times seem tougher.

Even though you can use AI to adopt different perspectives, it cannot replace the value of a rich professional network. It can't coach you through a difficult decision with full context. It can't introduce you to the person who becomes your next opportunity. And it can't provide the human connection that sustains you through hard stretches.

What You'll Practice

You'll map your network against SCAMP and fill one critical gap.

DAY 86 PRACTICE

Complete these exercises to build your SCAMP network:

1. MAP YOUR NETWORK

Create 5 columns: Skills, Coaching, Advice, Mentoring, Peer Support. Under each, write the names of people who genuinely provide that type of support. Be honest. Leave a column empty if you don't have coverage there. Don't list someone just to fill space.

2. IDENTIFY YOUR BIGGEST GAP

Look at your map. Which area is weakest or completely empty? Write down why this gap matters: what becomes harder without this support? How has lacking it already affected you?

3. FILL ONE GAP

Identify one person who could help fill your biggest gap. This might be someone you know but haven't asked, or someone you need to meet. Write down the person's name and one action you'll take this week to start building that relationship.

Reflection: *Which element of SCAMP would most accelerate your growth right now?*

DAY 87: STAY AHEAD OF AI_

AI CAPABILITIES ARE ADVANCING FASTER than most people realize. Features that seemed futuristic months ago are now standard. Tools that were cutting-edge last year feel basic today. And the rate of change will only increase.

You don't have to predict exactly what's coming to stay ahead, but you do need to build habits that help you spot and adapt to changes quickly. That includes regularly experimenting with new AI tools, following developments in your industry, and maintaining a network of people who share insights.

Why Does This Matter?

Most people react to technology changes long after they happen. They wait until a new tool is everywhere before learning it and update their skills only when forced to. That reactive approach could work reasonably well when change was slower.

It doesn't work anymore.

The goal isn't to be first to adopt every new technology. Instead, it is to ensure you're never completely caught off guard. When something significant shifts, you want to be among the people who adapt quickly, not among those scrambling to catch up months later.

What You'll Practice

You'll research AI developments relevant to one of your work tasks.

DAY 87 PRACTICE

Complete these exercises to build your early warning system:

1. AUDIT YOUR CURRENT AWARENESS

How do you currently learn about AI developments? List your sources: newsletters, podcasts, people you follow, communities you're part of. Be honest about how often you actually engage with these sources.

2. IDENTIFY GAPS

Ask AI: "What are the most significant AI developments in [your industry] in the last 6 months?" Compare what AI mentions to what you already know. Where are your blind spots?

3. BUILD YOUR SYSTEM

Design a simple routine for staying current. Include: one newsletter or source to check weekly, one new AI tool to experiment with monthly, one person to talk to about AI developments quarterly. Write down your specific commitments.

Reflection: *What's the cost of falling behind on AI developments in your field?*

DAY 88: WHAT'S COMING FOR YOUR INDUSTRY_

EVERY INDUSTRY IS BEING RESHAPED by AI, but not in the same way or at the same pace. Some roles and sectors are seeing rapid transformation while others are changing more gradually.

Of course, you won't be able to predict the future precisely for your role, your company and your industry, but now that you have a bigger picture view of AI, you can combine it with your domain specific knowledge. This will allow you to think forward, identify the most likely changes and position yourself to benefit from them.

Why Does This Matter?

By thinking specifically about your industry, you will prepare intelligently rather than anxiously. Will a variant of your role be relevant or not? Is your entire industry threatened? This type of knowledge will allow you to make smarter decisions about what to learn, what to double down on, and what to let go of.

What You'll Practice

You'll analyze AI's specific impact on your industry and role.

DAY 88 PRACTICE

Complete these exercises to understand your industry's AI trajectory:

1. MAP CURRENT AI IMPACT

List three ways AI is already affecting your industry today. Be specific: which companies are using it? Which processes have changed? Which roles have evolved?

2. GET AI'S PERSPECTIVE

Ask AI: "What are the most significant ways AI is expected to transform [your industry] in the next 3-5 years? What skills will become more valuable? What roles might change or disappear?" Compare AI's analysis to your own observations.

3. POSITION YOURSELF

Based on what you learned, identify: one skill you should develop, one part of your current role that will become more important, and one area where you should reduce your investment. Write down specific actions for each.

Reflection: *How does industry-specific thinking change your approach to AI preparation?*

DAY 89: YOU'RE
READY FOR ANYTHING_

You started this program with some level of AI awareness. But by now you should have discovered something far more important: the impact of AI on you, your team, and your organization. You can now think much more clearly about what the AI-Ready Human is, what the AI-Ready YOU is.

Once you truly master the Magnificent Seven capabilities in the context of an AI world, you will be able to look the future squarely in the eyes, and be ready for **whatever** it is.

Do you feel like you *are* nailing all seven, by now? If you still have concerns about a higher-level capability, remember, the source may be one of the lower-level ones. You might struggle for motivation because you don't bring focused energy. You may struggle to maintain control due to a lack of organization. In other words, "skipping layers" out of impatience won't help you.

Why Does This Matter?

AI will make all easily defined parts of work easier, to the point that humans might not be needed for many of them. What's left is the *intangibles*. This is why the World Economic Forum estimates that the number of jobs requiring advanced durable skills is expected to quadruple in the next decade.

What You'll Practice

You'll assess where you now stand on each of the Magnificent Seven capabilities and identify what needs most attention.

DAY 89 PRACTICE

Complete these exercises to assess your AI-readiness:

1. RATE YOURSELF

Go through each of the seven capabilities: Readiness, Organization, Control, Balance, Motivation, Resilience and Adaptability. For each one, honestly rate yourself: strong, developing, or needs work. Don't overthink it. Your gut reaction is probably accurate.

2. FIND YOUR WEAKEST LINK

Look at your ratings. Which capability is holding you back most? Now ask yourself: is the real problem actually a lower-level capability? If you rated Motivation as weak, could the root cause be Readiness? If Control feels shaky, might it stem from Organization gaps? Write down both the symptom and what you think the underlying cause might be.

3. REVIEW YOUR DAY 1

Go back and read what you wrote on Day 1 when you imagined your 2035 self. How did you think about AI then versus now? What's changed in your understanding? Write down the biggest shift in how you see AI's role in your work and life.

Reflection: *Which capability needs the most attention, and what might be underneath it?*

DAY 90: THE JOURNEY CONTINUES_

NINETY DAYS. That's what you've invested in becoming AI-ready. But this isn't the end. It can't be, because the only way you retain these capabilities is by continuing to work on them.

The good news is that the Magnificent Seven capabilities give you a structure that you can continuously work on. Remember, the capabilities themselves are evergreen, but the context in which you must apply them is ever-changing.

Tomorrow's AI will be different from today's, but by working on your capabilities daily, you will be ready for it.

Why Does This Matter?

What you do with your new understanding is up to you. Now might be the time to go deep on specific skills you've realized you are missing, to go deep on one or two of the areas you've found most interesting. Or you might even decide to go all the way back to Day One and start again.

Yes, really.

If you started reading this book three months ago, AI is different than when you started.

And you are different too.

But whatever you do, don't stop working on your capabilities. The world of work will never stand still, so stopping is really just moving backwards.

Congratulations for reaching this point, and here's to always being AI-ready

What You'll Practice

You'll choose your path forward and commit to ongoing practice.

DAY 90 PRACTICE

Complete these exercises to launch your ongoing journey:

1. CHOOSE YOUR PATH

Based on yesterday's self-assessment, decide what comes next. Will you go deep on a specific capability that needs work? Revisit the sections that resonated most? Or start again from Day 1 with fresh eyes and three months of AI change to incorporate? Write down your choice and why.

2. YOUR ONGOING COMMITMENTS

Write down three specific practices you'll continue: one daily practice (perhaps 10 minutes of reflective learning), one weekly practice (perhaps reviewing your week with AI), and one monthly practice (perhaps reassessing your capabilities). Be specific enough that you'll actually do them.

3. CELEBRATE AND SHARE

You've invested significant time and effort in this program. That deserves recognition. Tell someone what you've learned: a colleague, a friend, your manager. Or post about it. Sharing reinforces learning and might help someone else start their own journey.

Reflection: *What does being AI-ready mean to you now?*

AFTERWORD_

Thank you for reading this book.

Besides figuring out what is needed to be an AI-ready human, I hope that you are now thinking much more deeply about the role AI is playing in the world at large. Sure, AI is a tool, but it's really way more than that. Over the years I've been researching, writing and talking about AI, I've come to think of it as part tool, part significant other and part addictive drug. AI is not just changing work; it's changing society. It's helping us find cures for diseases while altering our minds to potentially increase our stupidity. It's supporting and accelerating human creativity while drowning out human voices with AI slop. And it has the potential to give us innovative solutions to the climate crisis while contributing massively to that very crisis with its hunger for power.

In an AI-world, everything is accelerated. Everything is turned up to eleven.

So, as a society, we have choices to make. Do we rush forward as fast as possible to an AI-dominant future, because if we don't another country will beat us? Do we allow AI to drown out human creativity because if we don't the stock market might take a hit? Do we put the power of AI in the hands of half a dozen tech bros, because (for now) they are "our" tech bros?

And as an individual, you have choices to make too. Do you stay firmly in control of your relationship with AI and use it to make you a smarter, more empathetic and more creative human? Do you ignore it? Or do let it wash over you as you doom scroll, and gradually slide into irrelevance, because anything else seems like hard work?

Look, I don't know where this is going, and I would urge you to be wary of anyone who claims they do. But I do know one thing. The most recent waves of technology innovation have been about more than productivity. For the first time, we are in a position where our value as human beings is being threatened, while a lot of us are asleep at the wheel.

So, let's pause for a moment, because the most important part of being an AI-ready human is not the AI part.

Human is Your Superpower.

ABOUT THE AUTHOR_

Paul Slater began his career as a technologist and learning and development professional in Oxford, England, in the 1990s, teaching office workers to use Microsoft Windows and productivity tools, and was the first recipient of the Microsoft UK Trainer of the Year Award. He started his own training, consulting and writing company (Entrace Technologies) with clients that included Dell Technologies, HP and Shell. Paul spent over a decade at Microsoft, where he was the ghostwriter of over a dozen books, more than twenty courses, and over a hundred white papers. He has served on AI-focused think tanks at Harvard University, Duke University and Arizona State University. In 2020 he founded BillionMinds, where he created the first example of personal effectiveness software, and built programs focused on building human skills for the future of work, used by thousands of employees worldwide.

Today, Paul is the founder and creative director of Humanity Working–a newsletter and podcast focused on bringing together voices who believe that the future of work must be human. He divides his time between writing, public speaking, consulting, and following the trials and tribulations of the England cricket team.

He lives in Tulsa, Oklahoma, with his wife (Anna), son (Orson), and dog (Jimmy).